# Toward the Next
# Economics

# Toward the Next Economics
# and Other Essays

Peter F. Drucker

Harvard Business Press

*Boston, Massachusetts*

Copyright 2010 Harvard Business School Publishing Corporation

Printed in the United States of America

14 13 12 11 10          5 4 3 2 1

Library-of-Congress cataloging information forthcoming
ISBN: 978-1-4221-3155-8

The paper used in this publication meets the requirements of the American National Standard for Permanence of Paper for Publications and Documents in Libraries and Archives Z39.48-1992.

# CONTENTS

# PREFACE

These twelve essays have a common author and a common point of view. And though their topics are diverse, all are concerned with "social ecology," and especially with the institutions—whether governments or organized science, businesses or schools—through which human beings attempt to realize values, traditions, and beliefs, and through which most people—and especially today's educated people—gain access to livelihood and achievement, to careers, and to standing in society. All these essays also share the conviction that sometime in the last decade there have been genuine structural changes in the "social ecology," most pronounced perhaps in population structure and population dynamics in the developed countries; but also in the role and performance of old-established and seemingly stable social bodies, such as government agencies or boards of directors, whether of businesses, hospitals, or universities; in the interface between sciences and society; and in fundamental theories that are still widely taught as "revealed truths."

This is thus a "contemporary" book that addresses itself to current concerns such as the environment, retirement policies in aging populations, or the impacts of technology. Yet, in selecting the pieces for this volume from my writings of the last ten years, I have excluded whatever might be called an article, that is, topical journalism, and have tried to confine myself to essays. To my mind, the difference is not one of style or length or level, but of intent. A good article catches the reality behind it, but it is concerned with the "here and now." The concerns to which these essays address themselves are those of the time in which they were written—our time. The intention in every one was however to use the moment to gain understanding, to project, to see to the permanent through the transient. This, I believe, is most apparent in the two essays that open and close the book, "Toward the Next Economics" and "A View of Japan Through Japanese Art." But the others are also informed by the same intent, and, I very much hope, convey to the reader the experience of self-knowledge, of immediacy, of direct understanding that a good portrait conveys, even though its subject may have been dead for centuries.

Most of the essays deal with concerns and challenges that are worldwide, or at least common to all developed non-Communist countries (and by and large to developed Communist countries as well). But since they were written in America, by an American and for publication in American journals, they heavily use American examples or figures. Only one piece however might be a little strange to non-American readers: the essay "Science and Industry: Challenges of Antagonistic Interdependence," which was delivered to the 1979 annual meeting of the American Association for the Advancement of Science. In writing this essay, I became aware of the extraordinary differences in the way in which various countries have structured the relationship between organized "big" science and society. To a German, the friction between the two in today's America must appear childish; to an Englishman or Japanese, on the contrary, the constant interaction between the two, however friction-laden, almost beyond belief. And all three might find it hard to accept that in an America renowned for its pragmatism, organized "official" Science has for a century indulged itself in an

extreme of virginal purity. Yet the concern of the essay: the growing divergence between the mind-sets and value systems of the
producers of scientific knowledge, the scientists, and the users and
consumers of scientific knowledge, government and industry, is
just as pronounced in all other developed countries and presents
just as great a threat, especially to science.

Two of the essays deal, however, with a special area rather than
with worldwide developments and problems: the last two essays
on Japan. It is a country in which I have been interested for almost
fifty years and which I have now visited more than a dozen times.
One fascination Japan holds for me is precisely that it is so different,
that it is indeed *sui generis*. It is no more "Asiatic" than it is
"Western"—and yet sometimes it is both. Few of what historians,
sociologists, or theorists consider "universal laws" hold for Japan.
Alone of all civilizations, it knew no property in land (except by
temples and the Emperor) until a hundred years ago; it knew only
rights to the land's products. Alone of all civilizations, it voluntarily
closed itself off from intercourse with the outside world for more
than two centuries, while yet maintaining the liveliest interest
in the arts, the learning, and the technology of the outside world,
and the greatest respect for it. Alone of all civilizations, it knew no
wars, whether external or internal, for more than two centuries,
even though being governed during that period by a military dicta-
torship and living under a code of martial ethics. Above all, of all
countries and civilizations I know of, Japan alone is accessible primarily through the eye rather than through the mind—and this
despite being, for long centuries, from 1600 until the late nineteenth
century, the country of the highest literacy rate. The last essay in
this volume thus represents an attempt at gaining through perception, via design and the visual arts, the same access to Japan and the
same understanding that one gains to other nations and other cultures through analysis, whether of philosophers or of institutions.
Whether the attempt is successful, the reader must judge; but it is

surely important—Japan is too important in the world today not to be perceived by us in the West. And if this essay will move even a few Western—or Japanese—readers to look at Japanese paintings, either when next they visit a museum or in one of the many excellent art books now available, I—and they—will be amply repaid.

Essays 2 to 10 are reprinted in chronological order; it seemed the easiest and least contrived. The opening essay is quite recent, however. My long-time editor at Harper & Row, Cass Canfield, Jr., suggested it be put first, as it deals with a subject likely to be of most interest to the widest spectrum of readers and yet normally rendered unintelligible, even to the highly educated among them, by the economists' propensity for technical jargon. And essay 11 is more recent still. It was written after my last trip to Japan in the summer of 1980, to answer all the many questions in the West about Japan's sweep into industrial leadership, all the questions about the "secret" of Japan's success. And it seemed only logical then to put essay 12, "A View of Japan Through Japanese Art," next to Essay 11 and at the very end.

In an essay volume there is always a temptation to rewrite. I have resisted it. All I have done is to clear up a few ambiguities. Where, for instance, an essay written in 1978 talked of "last fall," I have changed this to "1977," but have not changed anything else. I think it only fair to let the reader decide how well the author's opinions, prejudices, and predictions have stood the test of time. One essay, however, I have had to revise extensively: that on "A View of Japan Through Japanese Art." Originally, this piece was my contribution to the catalogue "Song of the Brush," which John M. Rosenfield of Harvard and Henry Trubner of the Seattle Art Museum edited for a major exhibition of Japanese paintings shown in 1979 and 1980 in New York; Cambridge, Massachusetts; Denver; San Francisco; and Seattle. The essay contained numerous references to paintings shown in the exhibition and illustrated in the catalogue, which have had to be deleted. The words that replace them are a poor substitute for pictures in a singularly beautiful catalogue, but the meaning still comes across, I trust.

This is my third volume of essays; the two earlier ones, containing selections spanning thirty years of writing each, were published respectively by Harper & Row in New York and by William Heinemann in London: *Technology, Management & Society* in 1970 and *Men, Ideas & Politics* in 1971. Both volumes were well received and gained a wide circle of readership, in the original hard-cover editions and, more recently, as paperbacks. I can only hope that this present volume will similarly renew many old and make many new friendships for me. For to a writer, even the most critical reader is a friend.

Peter F. Drucker
*Claremont, California*
*New Year's Day, 1981*

# CHAPTER ONE

# Toward the Next Economics

IN ITS FOUR-HUNDRED-YEAR HISTORY economics has passed through four major changes in its world view, its concerns, its paradigms. It is now in the throes of another, its fifth "scientific revolution."

Economics today is very largely "The House that Keynes Built." Even in the English-speaking world only a minority of economists are Keynesians in their specific theories. But the great majority, perhaps even in the Communist countries, are Keynesians in their "mind-set," in what they see and consider important, in their concerns, in their basic assumptions. They tend to define themselves largely through their relationship to Keynesian economics, are "near Keynesians" or "non-Keynesians" or "anti-Keynesians." Their terminology—Gross National Product, for instance, or money supply—assumes the economic aggregates on which Keynesian economics is based. The views of economic activity, economic policy, economic theory which Keynes around 1930 propounded—or at least codified—have, fifty years later, become the familiar environment, the home-ground of economists regardless of persuasion.

---

First published in *The Crisis in Economic Theory*, a special 1980 issue of *The Public Interest*.

The Keynesians may not muster the biggest battalions. But they have occupied the commanding heights and thereby define the issues.

Yet both as economic theory and as economic policy Keynesian economics is in disarray. It is unable to tackle the central policy problems of the developed economies—productivity and capital formation; indeed, Keynesian economics must deny that these problems could even exist. Nor is it able to provide theory that can encompass, let alone explain, observed economic reality and experience. And it has been proven to be entirely irrelevant to the economic needs and challenges of developing Third World countries, if not harmful to them.

Indeed, the two theoretical approaches which alone during these last ten or fifteen years have shown consistent predictive power are both incompatible with the Keynesian model: the theories of the Canadian-born Columbia University economist Robert Mundell, and those of the "rational expectations" school. Mundell, after thorough empirical studies, concluded more than ten years ago that Keynesian policies do not work in the international economy. He correctly predicted the failure of currency devaluations to correct the balance of payments, stem inflation, and improve competitive position. The "rational expectations" school goes even further; it postulates that governmental, that is, macro-economic, intervention is not just deleterious; it is futile and ineffectual.

But these new approaches are equally incompatible with pre-Keynesian theories, whether Neo-Classic or Marxist. What makes the present "crisis of economics" a genuine "Scientific Revolution" is our inability to go back to the economic world view which Keynes overturned. To be sure, most of the economic theorems, economic methodologies, economic terms found in the textbooks today will be found in the textbooks tomorrow. They will only be reinterpreted—the way quantum physics reinterprets Newton's Optics. After all, Keynes did not discard a single theorem of classical economics. He even retained "Say's Law," according to which savings always equal investments; it became a "special case." And one of the most advanced tools of modern economics, Input-Output Analysis, goes back to the first attempt at economic analysis, the Physiocrats' *Tableau Economique* more than two centuries ago. But as economic world view, or as economic system, the earlier theories—e.g., the disciplined orthodoxy of the "Austrians"—will not do. What made Keynes so compelling fifty years ago even to a doubter (as I must confess myself to have been even then) was the new vision he forced on us; we suddenly had to see a whole new reality—and that reality is still with us and will not disappear. The Next Economics will be "post-Keynesian." It cannot ignore Keynes, but it will have to transcend him.

There may be no "Economics" in the future. Totalitarian regimes, while greatly concerned with the economy, do not tolerate the postulate on which any discipline of economics must base itself: economic activity, though constrained and limited by non-economic rationality, concerns, and values, constitutes a discrete and separate sphere. Totalitarian regimes cannot accept economic activity as autonomous, internally consistent, and *"zweckrational"* within its boundaries. In a totalitarian regime, economics inexorably becomes a branch of accounting.

But if there is a future economics, it will differ fundamentally from the present one. We do not yet know what the economic theories of tomorrow will be. But we do know what the main problems, the main concerns, the main challenges will be. We do not know the Next Economics; but we can outline its specifications.


I


To do this, we have to look paradigmatically—that is, as methodologists rather than as economists—at the economic world views underlying the four "Scientific Revolutions" in economics that preceded the one in which we find ourselves, and especially at the basic world view and at the assumptions of the last, the Keynesian system.

Economics begins with the Cameralists and Mercantilists of France in the first half of the seventeenth century. They first saw the economy as autonomous. Earlier there was no economics, however great the concern with trade and livelihoods, with wealth, coinage, and taxes. As a system, a world view, Mercantilism was macro-economic and its universe was a political unit, the territory controlled by the Prince. Indeed the definition of the "national state," as it emerged at the end of the sixteenth century, was essentially an economic one: the unit controlled by the Prince through his control of coinage and foreign trade. Mercantilism was supply-focused economics. To produce the largest possible export surplus, and with it the hard currency needed to pay professional soldiers, was its central concern.

Despite its preoccupation with supply, Mercantilism failed however to produce it. Mercantilism collapsed as a system in what we would today call a "productivity crisis." The more the French government promoted manufacture for export and for the generation of specie, the poorer the country became—especially by contrast with the non-mercantilist, unsystematic, and unscientific English across the Channel. At the same time, Mercantilism also failed to spur capital formation. There were few economic statistics in those days other than foreign trade figures, the price of bread, and tax receipts; but there is no doubt that the French savings rate dropped sharply, while savings in non-mercantilist England steadily went up.

The Physiocrats started their "Scientific Revolution" with the paradox that under Mercantilism Europe's "richest country," France, had become one of its poorest ones, and was becoming the more wretched the more specie it earned. They solved the paradox by applying Gallic logic to Anglo-Saxon pragmatism. Their system remained as much supply-focused as was that of the Mercantilists. But they turned micro-economist, with the individual piece of land

and its cultivator the economic unit. This then forced them into the first economic theory of value—that is, the first theory that did not equate "wealth" with "money." The Physiocrats' source of value was nature in its economic manifestation, that is, land as producer of human sustenance. With this economics had become genuinely autonomous, had become a "discipline."

Classic Economics—the third of the economic world systems—took from the Physiocrats both the concern with supply and the focus on micro-economics. But it shifted the theory of value from "nature" to "man." With the Labor Theory of Values, economics became a "moral science." It is to this, as much as to its success in producing wealth, that Classic Economics owed its success and its rapid rise as the star amongst the new disciplines. But very soon, by the time of the mature John Stuart Mill in 1850 or so, the Labor Theory of Values became an impediment and the cause of serious theoretical turbulence.

This underlay the third of the Scientific Revolutions, the one that occurred in the second half of the nineteenth century: the shift from Classic to Neo-Classic economics, from the disciples of Ricardo to Leon Walras in Belgium and the Austrian pioneers of marginal utility. The shift was primarily philosophical. The Neo-Classics shifted from "value" to "utility." They shifted from human needs to human wants. They shifted from economic structure to economic analysis. To a non-economist this may not seem like a major shift, and may hardly deserve the name "Scientific Revolution." But it introduced a new spirit that has animated economics and economists alike to this day.

This third Scientific Revolution also split economics. Marx and the Marxists refused to abandon the Labor Theory of Value. This then forced them to spurn economic analysis. And they were forced also to subordinate economics to non-economic "historical forces." The Classics' micro-economics, with its built-in equilibrium, they asserted, would work only if and when meta-economic obstacles to labor's obtaining its full share of the social product would have been removed through political upheavals generated by the system's "economic contradictions"—or, as Lenin later redefined it, by the system's "political contradictions." Then the state would wither away, then micro-economics would take over: then there would be equilibrium.

Seen against the paradigmatic background of economics, Keynes was indeed right in the claim he voiced in his Cambridge seminar in the thirties that his economics represented a far more radical break with tradition than Marx and Marxism. Keynes not only went back to the Mercantilists in being macro-economic. He stood all earlier systems on their heads by being demand-centered rather than supply-centered. In all earlier economics, demand is a function of supply. In Keynesian economics, supply is a function of demand and controlled by it. Above all—the greatest innovation—Keynes redefined economic reality. Instead of goods, services, and work—realities of the physical world and "things"—Keynes' economic realities are symbols: money and credit. To the Mercantilists, too, money gave control—but political rather than economic control. Keynes was the first to postulate that money and credit give complete *economic* control.

The relationship between the "real" economy of goods, work, and services, and the "symbol" economy of money and credit had been a problem since earliest times. Few economists were satisfied with the way the Classics (following the Physiocrats) dismissed money as the "veil of reality." Well before Keynes, economists of stature, e.g., MacCulloch, otherwise a devout Ricardian, or, in the generation before Keynes, the Swede Karl Gustav Cassel and the German Georg Friedrich Knapp, had attempted to replace a thing-based economics with a symbol-based one. But it was Keynes' observation that in the recession of the 1920s the English labor unions treated money wages as "real" and as "income," even when this actually resulted in lower purchasing power for their members, that then produced a genuine "Scientific Revolution." In Keynesian economics commodities, production, work, are the "veil of reality." Or, rather, these *things* are determined by monetary events: money supply, credit, interest rates, and governmental surpluses or deficits. Goods, services, production, productivity, demand, employment, and finally prices, are all dependent variables of the macro-economic events of the monetary symbol economy. Philosophically speaking, Keynes became an extreme nominalist—it was perhaps not entirely coincidence that he and Wittgenstein were contemporaries at Cambridge.

Looked at paradigmatically, Milton Friedman is as much a "Keynesian" as the Master himself, rather than the "anti-Keynesian" as which he is commonly depicted. Friedman accepts without reservation the Keynesian world view. His economics is pure macro-economics, with the national government as the one unit, the one dynamic force, controlling the economy through the money supply. Friedman's economics are completely demand-focused. Money and credit are the pervasive, and indeed the only, economic reality. That Friedman sees money supply as original and interest rates as derivative, is not much more than minor gloss on the Keynesian scriptures. It is "fine-tuning" Keynes. And what has made Friedman stand out is not so much his monetary theory as his insistence on economic activity as being autonomous, on economic values as the hinge on which economic policy and behavior must turn, and on the free market—on all of which Keynes himself would have been in full agreement.

To Classics, Neo-Classics, and Marxists, the Great Depression of the 1930s originated in the "real economy," in the impoverishment of Europe in World War I, further aggravated by Reparations and by a sharp drop in the productivity of European agriculture and industry. To a Keynesian, however, including Friedman, the Great Depression was the result of the Stock Exchange crash of 1929, of "speculation," or of a contraction in the money supply, that is, of events in the symbol-economy.

## II

The present "crisis in economics" is a failure of the basic assumptions, of the paradigm, of the "system," rather than of this or that theory. Keynesian economics has run into the most severe productivity crisis since that of France in the eighteenth century which discredited Mercantilism. This productivity crisis in all developed countries—and worst in the two most faithfully Keynesian countries, Great Britain and the United States—invalidates the Keynesian theorem of the demand-control of supply. The crisis in capital formation which we are facing at the same time—again at its worst in Great Britain and the United States—could not, within Keynesian economics, have happened at all; it is theoretically impossible within the Keynesian paradigms.

Keynes was fully aware of the importance of productivity. But he was also convinced that productivity is a function of demand and determined by it. In the early thirties, the great years of the Keynes seminar in Cambridge, one heard again and again of Keynes being asked by one of the first-rate minds in the seminar, Joan Robinson perhaps or Roy Harrod, or Abba Lerner, "What about productivity?" He always answered: "We can take productivity for granted, provided that employment and demand remain high."

The Classics had not taken productivity for granted. On the contrary, central to classical economics is the "law" of the diminishing return of all resources. Marx had based his forecast of the imminent demise of the "bourgeois system" (the term "capitalism" was not coined until after Marx's death) on this axiom. What made Marx different was only his meta-economic, semi-religious belief that the end of "alienation" would release such enormous human energy as to reverse the diminishing return on resources in an outburst of "creativity." But just when Marx, in the last unfinished volume of Das Kapital, most confidently predicted the demise of the "system" because of its inherent productivity crisis, productivity began to go up sharply. In part this was the result of the systematic approach to work, first developed by Frederick W. Taylor in his "Task Study" (only later misnamed "Scientific Management"),* which showed that human work can be made infinitely more productive, not by "working harder" but by "working smarter." In part this was the result of the great age of innovations, both in technology and in business and management (e.g., installment buying), as a result of which resources were systematically shifted from older and less productive into newer and more productive employments. In large part, the rise in productivity was the result of steady work on making resources— especially capital—more productive. The greatest productivity increase in the last hundred years has probably not been in the factory, but in commercial banking, where one dollar of assets today supports at least a hundred times the volume of transaction it supported a hundred years ago—and without any release of "creativity" or any great innovation. At that time—that is, in the decades around 1900—the developed countries learned to use capital not to replace labor, but to upgrade it and to make it more productive, as Simon Kuznets of Harvard has shown in his pioneering studies for which he received the Nobel Prize in Economics. Altogether, the reversal of the theory of productivity between 1900 and 1920 from one that postulated a built-in tendency toward diminishing returns to one that postulated a steady increase, was a major factor in the Keynesian "Scientific Revolution." It made possible, in large measure, the shift from supply-focus to demand-focus, that is, to the belief that production tends inherently to surplus rather than to scarcity.

It was thus not totally frivolous to assume as Keynes did, fifty years ago, that productivity would take care of itself and would continue to increase slowly but steadily, if only economic confidence prevailed for both businessmen and workingmen, if only demand kept high and unemployment low. In the early thirties Keynes' was a rational—albeit optimistic—view (though even then Joseph Schumpeter and Lionel Robbins could not accept it).

---

*On this, see "The Coming Rediscovery of Scientific Management."

But surely this can no longer be maintained. And yet within the Keynesian system there is no room for productivity, no way to stimulate or to spur it, no means to make an economy more productive. With productivity emerging as a central economic need and problem, especially in the most highly developed countries—and a need alike in manufacturing, in services, and in agriculture—the Keynesian inability to handle productivity within the theoretical structure or within economic policy is as serious a flaw as was the inability of Ptolemaic astronomy around the time of Copernicus to explain the motion of stars and planets.

For economic theory, the decline in capital formation in the developed countries, and especially in the countries of the Keynesian true believers—that is, in the United States and Great Britain—is even more serious. Within Keynesian economics the decline cannot be explained, cannot have happened.

Capital is the future. It is the provision for the risks, the uncertainties, the changes, and the jobs of tomorrow. It is not "present" cost—but it is certain cost. An economy that does not form enough capital to cover its future costs is an economy that condemns itself to decline and continuing crisis, the crisis of "stagflation," in which—an impossibility for both Neo-Classics and Keynesians—there is simultaneously both high unemployment and inflation.

The essence of Keynesian economic theory, as every undergraduate is being taught, was the repudiation of "Say's Law," according to which Savings always equal Investment, so that an economy always forms enough capital for its future needs. Keynes postulated instead a tendency toward "over-saving" for developed economies. "Under-saving," that is, a shortfall in capital formation, cannot possibly occur in a developed economy according to the Keynesian postulates. From the beginning this was seen as a serious flaw in Keynesian economics by such thoughtful (and sympathetic) critics as Joseph Schumpeter, Surely, once it is accepted that savings and investment need not be identical, "under-saving" is just as likely as "over-saving." And what we have had in the last thirty years in the

English-speaking, developed, that is, the Keynesian, countries—beginning well before the energy crisis—is "under-saving" on a massive scale. The basic assumption underlying the Keynesian paradigm can therefore no longer be held or defended. Within the Keynesian economic universe, however, capital formation cannot be dealt with. Keynesian economics explicitly excludes the possibility of under-saving, and thereby of inadequate capital formation. And if capital is a true "cost" of the economy—and even Keynes never doubted this—demand-based macro-economics cannot adequately deal with economic theory or economic policy.

Even the Keynesian assertion that consumer demand can be managed by managing money incomes and interest rates macro-economically is not supported by the experience of the last forty years. The one example which the Keynesians always cite for the success of their approach, the "Kennedy tax cut" of the early sixties, proves nothing. The American economy did indeed experience a significant upturn in the year in which the Kennedy administration cut federal taxes. But in that same year state and local taxes in the United States went up so sharply as to offset the federal tax cut. There is nothing in Keynesian theory or in economic reality that would explain why state and local taxes differ in their economic impact from federal taxes.* And the other examples of the effect of Keynesian policies actually disprove the claim that the economy can be managed macro-economically through the stimulus of lower interest rates or larger government deficits. Both in the New Deal years in the United States and in those of the British "stagflation" since 1960, larger government deficits failed to stimulate supply. Their effect was nullified by micro-economic sabotage, that is, by a sharp slowing down of the velocity of money-turnover and by

---

*For this reason also, the "Kennedy tax cut" does not, as has sometimes been asserted, prove or support the "Laffer Curve" and its thesis that lower tax *rates* will, beyond a certain point, actually produce higher taxes because they stimulate greater economic activity. The "Kennedy tax cut," precisely because there was no such "tax cut," proves nothing and disproves nothing.

a drop in investment—neither of which could have happened if macro-economics really determined micro-economic attitudes, behavior, and actions, as Keynes postulated.

Even more serious may be the failure of the basic philosophical foundation of Keynesian economic *policy*: the belief in the "economist-king," the objective, independent expert who makes effective decisions based solely on impersonal, quantitative, unambiguous evidence, and free alike of political ambitions for himself and of political pressures on him. Even in the 1930s, a good many people found it difficult to accept this. To the Continental Europeans in particular, with their memories of the postwar inflations, the economist-king was sheer *hubris*—which in large measure explains why Keynes has had so few followers on the Continent until the last ten or fifteen years. By now, however, few would altogether swallow the non-political economist who, at the same time, controls crucial political decisions. Like "enlightened despots," the Keynesian "economist-king" has proven to be a delusion, and indeed a contradiction in terms. If there is one thing taught by the inflations of the last decade—as it was taught in the inflations of the twenties in Europe—it is that the economist in power either becomes himself a politician and expedient, if not irresponsible; or he soon ceases to have power and influence altogether. It is simply not true, as is often asserted, that economists do not know how to stop inflation. Every economist since the late sixteenth century has known how to do it: cut government expenses and with them the creation of money. What economists lack is not theoretical knowledge. It is political will or political power. And so far all inflations have been ended by politicians who had the will rather than by economists who had the knowledge.

Without the "economist-king," Keynesian economics ceases however to be operational. It can play the role of critic, which Keynes played in the 1920s and which Milton Friedman plays today. In opposition, the Keynesian economist, being powerless, can also be politics-free. But it is an opposition that cannot become effective government. The Keynesian paradigm is thus likely to be around a long time as a critique and as a guide to what not to do. But it is fast losing its credibility as a foundation for economic theory and as a guide to policy and action.

III

That there is both a productivity crisis and a capital-formation crisis makes certain that the Next Economics will have to be again micro-economic and centered on supply. Both productivity and capital formation are events of the micro-economy. Both also deal with the factors of *production* rather than being functions of demand.

We know a good deal about productivity and capital formation. A vast amount of empirical and of theoretical work has been done in either area these last thirty years. Productivity, we know, means both the economic yield from every one of the factors of production: the human resource, capital, physical resources, and time; and the overall yield of the joint resources in combination. Capital formation, we know, has to be at least equal to the cost of capital. And in a growing economy, the costs of the future to be covered by today's capital formation are substantially higher even than the cost of capital. In a growing economy, tomorrow's jobs, by definition, will require substantially higher capital investment than today's jobs, and will thus require substantially greater capital formation than the replacement of capital represented by the prevailing return rate for capital. And we know how to determine the rate of capital formation needed for the uncertainties of the future within a margin of error that is not greater than that which pertains to such accepted costs of the present in the accounting model as depreciation or credit risks.

We also know quite a bit about the factors and forces which encourage both greater productivity and greater capital formation. None of them, it should be said, is a factor of the "symbol economy" of money and credit. Events in the symbol economy can discourage, but are unlikely significantly to encourage either productivity or a higher rate of capital formation.

But while we have both the concepts and the data, we do not however have, so far, a micro-economic model that embraces productivity and capital formation. Even the terms are largely unknown to the available theories, e.g., the Theory of the Firm, which is the micro-economics most commonly taught in our college courses. Instead of productivity and capital formation, the Theory of the Firm talks of "profit maximization." But we have known for at least fifty years that "profit maximization" is a meaningless term if applied to anything other than a unique, non-recurrent trading transaction on the part of an individual and in a single commodity, that is, to an exceptional, rare, and quite unrepresentative incident. Altogether the Next Economics in its micro-economics will, almost certainly, discard the concept of "profit." It assumes a static, unchanging, closed economy. In a moving, changing, open-ended economy, in which there is risk, uncertainty, and change, there is no "profit," except—as Schumpeter taught seventy years ago—the temporary profit of the genuine innovator. For any other economic activity there is only cost—the costs of past and present, which are embodied in the accounting model, and the costs of the future expressed in the cost of capital. Indeed, no business is known to apply "profit maximization" to its planning or to its decisions on capital investment or pricing. The theories and concepts that govern the actual behavior of firms are theories of the cost of capital, of market optimization, and of the long-range cost gains (the "learning curve") from maximizing the volume of production rather than from maximizing profitability.

The next Economics will thus require radically different micro-economics as its foundation. It will require a theory that aims at *optimizing* productivity; for a balance of several partially dependent functions is, of necessity, an optimization rather than a maximization. Capital formation requires a minimum concept: the coverage of the cost of capital. It requires a theory that aims at "satisficing" rather than at maximizing profit (though the minimum cost of capital will, paradoxically, be found to be substantially higher than what most present-day economists and most business executives consider the available maximum profitability—which is, of course, why there is a "capital formation crisis"). The next micro-economics, unlike the present one, will be dynamic and assume risk, uncertainty, and change in technology, economic conditions, and markets. Yet it should be equilibrium economics, integrating a provision for an uncertain and changing future into present and testable behavior. Much of the spadework for this has already been done—in part, fifty years ago, by the Chicago economist Frank Knight; in part by the contemporary English economist G. L. S. Shackle. The next micro-economic theory should thus be able to resolve the dilemma that has plagued economists since Ricardo, almost two hundred years ago: economic analysis is possible only if it excludes uncertainty and change, and economic policy is possible only in contemplation of uncertainty and change. In the next micro-economics, we should be able to integrate both analysis and policy in one dynamic equilibrium through productivity and capital formation.

If productivity and capital formation are its focal points, a micro-economic theory can also do what never before could be done in economics: to tie together micro-economics and macro-economics, if not make them into one. While productivity and capital formation are events of the micro-economy, they are—unlike profit—meaningful terms of the macro-economy as well, and measurable macro-economic aggregates. "Profit," by definition, applies only to one legal entity, the "entrepreneur" or the "Firm." But it makes sense to speak of the productivity of an industry or of capital formation in the world economy.

In the past, economic theory was either micro-economic or macro-economic. Alfred Marshall, the last "Classic" economist, tried in the early years of this century to combine the two; but no one, including Marshall himself, thought that he had succeeded. And it was Marshall's failure, in large part, that made Keynes opt for a purely macro-economic system. The Next Economics will not, it is reasonably certain, have the luxury, however, of choosing between micro-economics and macro-economics. It will have to accomplish what Marshall tried and failed to do: integrate both. Macro-economics has proven itself—for the second time—to be unable to handle supply, that is, productivity and capital formation. Yet micro-economics alone is not adequate either for economic theory or for economic policy in a world of mixed economies, of multinational corporations, of non-convertible currencies, and of governments' redistributing half of their nation's income.

But what the term "macro-economy" will actually mean in the Next Economics is anything but clear and will be highly controversial. For four hundred years the term automatically meant the "national economy." The Germans, to this day, call the discipline of "economics" "Nationaloekonomie" or "Volkswirtschaft." But the one theory today which attempts to integrate micro-economics and macro-economics, that of Robert Mundell, all but dismisses national government as a factor. Mundell's macro-economy is the world economy. National governments, in Mundell's economics, are effective only insofar as they are agents of the world economy, anticipating its structural trends and shaping their own domestic economies to conform; the examples are Japan and Germany in the years of their most rapid growth in the sixties. And the countries that attempted to behave like true "macro-economies" during the post-World War II period—especially the Keynesian countries, Great Britain and the United States—are, as Mundell shows, also the countries that had the least control over their national economies and at the highest cost.

This, by the way, was the conclusion Keynes himself reached for toward the end of his life. Around 1942, Keynes ceased to be a "Keynesian" and abandoned the nation-state as the macro-economy. Instead he proposed to build the postwar economy around "Bancor," a transnational money that would be independent of national governments and national currencies and managed by non-political economists acting as transnational civil servants. "Bancor" was shot down at the Bretton Woods Conference by the American Keynesians, who suspected it of being an attempt to maintain the Pound Sterling as the world's "key currency," but who also were arrogantly confident of the ability of the American dollar to be the world's "key currency" and of the wisdom of American economists in managing the dollar and in keeping it free from domestic political pressures. But today even the Americans are pushing the "Special Drawing Rights" (SDR) of the International Monetary Fund as the transnational and non-national money of the world economy. Even the Americans have accepted that there can be no "key currency"—that is, that no nation-state can aspire to genuine economic sovereignty. And the major holders of liquid funds in the world economy—the OPEC countries, the major Central Banks, and the very large multinationals based in balance-of-payments surplus countries such as Germany, Japan, or Switzerland—are fast putting their cash into transnational money: the SDRs, a "market basket" of national currencies, money of account indexed to purchasing power, or gold.

And yet it makes sense to speak of a "Brazilian economy" or a "British economy." The nation-state is a reality. It is not *the* economic reality, the way traditional macro-economics has it. But it is also not an "extraneous factor," which can limit economic activity, but cannot determine or direct it. The Next Economics will have to account for this reality. For the national state is surely, for the foreseeable future, the one political institution around.

Predictably, therefore, the Next Economics will, at its center, have a spirited debate over the place of national government in economic theory. One approach might follow Mundell and consider the national government, at least in developed countries, to be no more than a gear in the system rather than its engine. Another approach, predictably, will attempt to maintain the nation-state and its government as the center of the economic universe, with both the macro-economy and the world economy, so to speak, planets in orbit around it. There may even be two parallel theorems of such a "Ptolemaic," "nation-centered" economic system, an Anglo-American and Neo-Keynesian one, and a French and Cameralist one—one approach attempting to maintain control and uniqueness of the national economy through money and credit, and the other one controlling through what the French call "indicative planning," that is, through allocation of capital, labor, and physical resources. There may be—methodologically there almost has to be—a further approach which tries to organize the three centers in one system, the micro-economics of the individual and the firm, the intermediate economics of the nation-state, and the macro-economics of the world economy. This, I would think, might be the only model adequate for developing countries, and especially for rapidly industrializing ones. In any event, the Next Economics will surely again be "political economy," with the question of the relationship between economic realities, that is, world economy and micro-economy, and political realities, that is, the nation-state, both central to economic theory and highly controversial.

Equally central, and perhaps even more controversial, will be the relationship between the "real economy" of things: commodities, resources, work, and the "symbol economy" of money and credit. There is no returning to the old dismissal of the symbol economy as the "veil of reality." But there is no holding on to the recent orthodoxy in which the symbol economy is the real and true economy, with things: commodities, services, and work, only "functions" and indeed totally dependent functions, of the "symbol economy."

We may have to be content, however, with something analogous to the physicist's "Uncertainty Principle," in which the only meaningful statements in respect to certain events—productivity, for instance, capital formation, the allocation of resources, and so on—are statements in terms of the "real economy," with events in the "symbol economy" a restraint and a boundary only. But other and equally "real" events can perhaps only be discussed, analyzed, and even described in terms of the "symbol economy," with the "real economy" of things being a restraint on them. This would not be particularly satisfactory—but it may be the best we can achieve.

## IV

No one today can predict whether the Next Economics will be designed by one great thinker, another Adam Smith, a Ricardo, or a Keynes; or whether it will emerge in a gradual shift, resulting from the work of a great many competent people, as did the shift from the Classic to the Neo-Classic Economics of marginal utility a century ago. The Next Economics may be a massive tower reared on one intellectual foundation, similar to the edifice Keynes designed half a century ago. Or it may be sprawling suburbia without a center, held together only by a number of busy super-highways. But the Next Economics will, of necessity, have to embody what in the history of economic thought were always discrete alternatives, if not opposites: micro-economy and macro-economy; the real economy of commodities and work and the symbol economy of money and credit. It will use for its building blocks the economic thought and the economic theories of the entire four hundred years of the history of economics; but it is quite unlikely to accept any one of them either as foundation or as capstone.

And the Next Economics may even attempt again to be both "humanity" and "science."

An anecdote popular among the younger members of Keynes' Cambridge seminar in the thirties had one of the disciples ask the Master why there was no Theory of Value in his *General Theory*. Keynes was said to have answered: "Because the only available Theory of Value is the Labor Theory, and it is totally discredited." The Next Economics may again have a Theory of Value. It may proclaim that productivity—that is, knowledge applied to resources through human work—is the source of all economic value.

Productivity as the source of value is both *a priori* and operational, and thus satisfies the specifications for a first principle. It would be both descriptive and normative, both describe what is and why and indicate what ought to be and why. Marx, as the "Revisionists" of socialism around 1900 used to argue, was never fully satisfied with the Labor Theory of Value, but groped in vain for a substitute. None of the great non-Marxist economists of the last hundred years, Alfred Marshall, Joseph Schumpeter, or John Maynard Keynes, was in turn comfortable with an economics that lacked a Theory of Value altogether. But, as the Keynes anecdote illustrates, they saw no alternative. Productivity as the source of all economic value would serve. It would explain. It would direct vision. It would give guidance to analysis, to policy and behavior. Productivity is both, man and things; both structural and analytical. A productivity-based economics might thus become what all great economists have striven for: both a "humanity," a "moral philosophy," a "*Geisteswissenschaft*"; and rigorous "science."

# CHAPTER TWO

# Saving the Crusade

## *The High Cost of Our Environmental Future*

EVERYBODY TODAY IS "FOR THE ENVIRONMENT."
Laws and agencies destined to protect it multiply at all levels of government. Big corporations take full-color ads to explain how they're cleaning up, or at least trying to. Even you as a private citizen probably make
some conscientious effort to curb pollution. At the same time, we have
learned enough about the problem to make some progress toward
restoring a balance between man and nature.

Yet the crusade is in real danger of running off the tracks, much
like its immediate predecessor, the so-called war on poverty. Paradoxically, the most fervent environmentalists may be among the
chief wreckers. Many are confused about the cause of our crisis
and the way in which we might resolve it. They ignore the difficult
decisions that must be made; they splinter the resources available
for attacking environmental problems. Indeed, some of our leading crusaders seem almost perversely determined to sabotage their
cause—and our future.

---

First published in *Harper's Magazine*, January 1972.

Consider, for example, the widespread illusion that a clean environment can be obtained by reducing or even abolishing our dependence on "technology." The growing pollution crisis does indeed raise fundamental questions about technology—its directions, uses, and future. But the relationship between technology and the environment is hardly as simple as much anti-technological rhetoric would have us believe. The invention that has probably had the greatest environmental impact in the past twenty-five years, for instance, is that seemingly insignificant gadget, the wire-screen window. The wire screen, rather than DDT or antibiotics, detonated the "population explosion" in underdeveloped countries, where only a few decades ago as many as four out of five children died of such insect-borne diseases as "summer diarrhea" or malaria before their fifth birthday. Would even the most ardent environmentalist outlaw the screen window and expose those babies again to the flies?

The truth is that most environmental problems require technological solutions—and dozens of them. To control our biggest water pollutant, human wastes, we will have to draw on all sciences and technologies from biochemistry to thermodynamics. Similarly, we need the most advanced technology for adequate treatment of the effluents that mining and manufacturing spew into the world's waters. It will take even more new technology to repair the damage caused by the third major source of water pollution in this country—the activities of farmers and loggers.

Even the hope of genuine disarmament—and the arms race may be our worst and most dangerous pollutant—rests largely on complex technologies of remote inspection and surveillance. Environmental control, in other words, requires technology at a level at least as high as the technology whose misuse it is designed to correct. The sewage-treatment plants that are urgently needed all over the world will be designed, built, and kept running not by purity of heart, ballads, or Earth Days but by crew-cut engineers working in very large organizations, whether businesses, research labs, or government agencies.

## Who Will Pay?

The second and equally dangerous delusion abroad today is the common belief that the cost of cleaning the environment can be paid for out of "business profits." After taxes, the profits of all American businesses in a good year come to sixty or seventy billion dollars. And mining and manufacturing—the most polluting industries—account for less than half of this. But at the lowest estimate, the cleanup bill, even for just the most urgent jobs, will be three or four times as large as all business profits.

Consider the most efficient and most profitable electric-power company in the country (and probably in the world): the American Power Company, which operates a number of large power systems in the Midwest and upper South. It has always been far more ecology-minded than most other power companies, including the government's own TVA. Yet cleaning up American Power's plants to the point where they no longer befoul air and water will require, for many years to come, an annual outlay close to, if not exceeding, the company's present annual profit of $100 million. The added expense caused by giving up strip mining of coal or by reclaiming strip-mined land might double the company's fuel bill, its single largest operating cost. No one can even guess what it would cost—if and when it can be done technologically—to put power transmission lines underground. It might well be a good deal more than power companies have ever earned.

We face an environmental crisis because for too long we have disregarded genuine costs. Now we must raise the costs, in a hurry, to where they should have been all along. The expense must be borne, eventually, by the great mass of the people as consumers and producers. The only choice we have is which of the costs will be borne in the form of higher prices, and which in the form of higher taxes.

It may be possible to convert part of this economic burden into economic opportunity, though not without hard work and, again, new technology. Many industrial or human wastes might be transformed into valuable products. The heat produced in generating electricity might be used in greenhouses and fish farming, or to punch "heat holes" into the layer of cold air over such places as Los Angeles, creating an updraft to draw off the smog. But these are long-range projects. The increased costs are here and now.

Closely related to the fallacy that "profit" can pay the environmental bill is the belief that we can solve the environmental crisis by reducing industrial output. In the highly developed affluent countries of the world, it is true that we may be about to deemphasize the "production orientation" of the past few hundred years. Indeed, the "growth sectors" of the developed economies are increasingly education, leisure activities, or health care rather than goods. But paradoxical as it may sound, the environmental crisis will force us to return for several decades to an emphasis on both growth and industrial output.

## Overlooked Facts of Life

There are three reasons for this, each adequate in itself.

1. Practically every environmental task demands huge amounts of electrical energy, way beyond anything now available. Sewage treatment is just one example: the difference between the traditional and wholly inadequate methods and a modern treatment plant that gets rid of human and industrial wastes and produces reasonably clear water is primarily electric power, and vast supplies of it. This poses a difficult dilemma. Power plants are themselves polluters. And one of their major pollution hazards, thermal pollution, is something we do not yet know how to handle.

Had we better postpone any serious attack on other environmental tasks until we have solved the pollution problems of electric-power generation? It would be a quixotic decision, but at least it would be a deliberate one. What is simply dishonest is the present hypocrisy that maintains we are serious about these other problems—industrial wastes, for instance, or sewage or pesticides—while we refuse to build the power plants we need to resolve them. I happen to be a member of the Sierra Club, America's oldest and largest environmental group. I share its concern for the environment. But the Sierra Club's opposition to any new power plant today—and the opposition of other groups to new power plants in other parts of the country (e.g., New York City)—has, in the first place, ensured that other ecological tasks cannot be done effectively for the next five or ten years. Secondly, it has made certain that the internal combustion engine is going to remain our mainstay in transportation for a long time to come. An electrical automobile or electrified mass transportation—the only feasible alternatives—would require an even more rapid increase in electrical power than any now projected. And thirdly, it may well, a few years hence, cause power shortages along the Atlantic Coast, which would mean unheated homes in winter, as well as widespread industrial shutdowns and unemployment. This would almost certainly start a "backlash" against the whole environmental crusade.

2. No matter how desirable a deemphasis on production might be, the next decade is the wrong time for it in all the developed countries and especially in the United States. The next decade will bring a surge in employment-seekers and in the formation of young families—both the inevitable result of the baby boom of the late forties and early fifties. Young adults need jobs; and unless there is a rapid expansion of jobs in production there will be massive unemployment, especially of low-skilled blacks and other minority group members. In addition to jobs, young families

need goods—from housing and furniture to shoes for the baby. Even if the individual family's standard of consumption goes down quite a bit, total demand—barring only a severe depression—will go up sharply. If this is resisted in the name of ecology, environment will become a dirty word in the political vocabulary.

3. If there is no expansion of output equal to the additional cost of cleaning up the environment, the cost burden will—indeed, must—be met by cutting the funds available for education, health care, or the inner city, thus depriving the poor. It would be nice if the resources we need could come out of defense spending. But of the 6 or 7 percent of our national income that now goes for defense, a large part is cost of past wars, that is, veterans' pensions and disability benefits (which, incidentally, most other countries do not include in their defense budgets—a fact critics of "American militarism" often ignore). Even if we could—or should—cut defense spending, the "peace dividend" is going to be 1 or 2 percent of national income, at best.

   But the total national outlay for education (7 to 8 percent), health care (another 7 to 8 percent), and the inner city and other poverty areas (almost 5 percent) comes to a fifth of total national income today. Unless we raise output and productivity fast enough to offset the added environmental cost, the voters will look to this sector for money. Indeed, in their rejection of school budgets across the nation and in their desperate attempts to cut welfare costs, voters have already begun to do so. That the shift of resources is likely to be accomplished in large part through infla- tion—essentially at the expense of the lower-income groups—will hardly make the environmental cause more popular with the poor.

   The only way to avoid these evils is to expand the economy, probably at a rate of growth on the order of 4 percent a year for the next decade, a higher rate than we have been able to sustain in this country in the postwar years. This undoubtedly entails very great environmental risks. But the alternative is likely to mean no environmental action at all, and a rapid public turn—by no means confined to the "hard hats"—against all environmental concern whatever.

## Making Virtue Pay

The final delusion is that the proper way to bring about a clean environment is through punitive legislation. We do need prohibitions and laws forbidding actions that endanger and degrade the environment. But more than that, we need incentives to preserve and improve it.

Punitive laws succeed only if the malefactors are few and the unlawful act is comparatively rare. Whenever the law attempts to prevent or control something everybody is doing, it degenerates into a huge but futile machine of informers, spies, bribe givers, and bribe takers. Today every one of us—in the underdeveloped countries almost as much as in the developed ones—is a polluter. Punitive laws and regulations can force automobile manufacturers to put emission controls into new cars, but they will never be able to force 100 million motorists to maintain this equipment. Yet this is going to be the central task if we are to stop automotive pollution.

What we should do is make it to everyone's advantage to reach environmental goals. And since the roots of the environmental crisis are so largely in economic activity, the incentives will have to be largely economic ones as well. Automobile owners who voluntarily maintain in working order the emission controls of their cars might, for instance, pay a much lower automobile registration fee, while those whose cars fall below accepted standards might pay a much higher fee. And if they were offered a sizable tax incentive, the automobile companies would put all their best energies to work to produce safer and emission-free cars, rather than fight delaying actions against punitive legislation.

Despite all the rhetoric on the campuses, we know by now that "capitalism" has nothing to do with the ecological crisis, which is fully as severe in the Communist countries. The bathing beaches for fifty miles around Stockholm have become completely unusable because of the raw, untreated sewage from Communist Leningrad that drifts across the narrow Baltic. Moscow, even though it still has few automobiles, has as bad an air-pollution problem as Los Angeles—and has done less about it so far.

We should also know that "greed" has little to do with the environmental crisis. The two main causes are population pressures, especially the pressures of large metropolitan populations, and the desire—a highly commendable one—to bring a decent living at the lowest possible cost to the largest possible number of people.

The environmental crisis is the result of success—success in cutting down the mortality of infants (which has given us the population explosion), success in raising farm output sufficiently to prevent mass famine (which has given us contamination by insecticides, pesticides, and chemical fertilizers), success in getting people out of the noisome tenements of the nineteenth-century city and into the greenery and privacy of the single-family home in the suburbs (which has given us urban sprawl and traffic jams). The environmental crisis, in other words, is very largely the result of doing too much of the right sort of thing.

To overcome the problems success always creates, one has to build on it. The first step entails a willingness to take the risks involved in making decisions about complicated and perilous dilemmas:

- What is the best "trade-off" between a cleaner environment and unemployment?
- How can we prevent the environmental crusade from becoming a war of the rich against the poor, a new and particularly vicious "white racist imperialism"?

- What can we do to harmonize the worldwide needs of the environment with the political and economic needs of other countries, and to keep Western leadership from becoming Western aggression?
- How can we strike the least agonizing balance of risks between environmental damage and mass starvation of poor children, or between environmental damage and large-scale epidemics?

## An Environmental Crime?

More than twenty years ago, three young chemical engineers came to seek my advice. They were working for one of the big chemical companies, and its managers had told them to figure out what kind of new plants to put into West Virginia, where poverty was rampant. The three young men had drawn up a long-range plan for systematic job creation, but it included one project about which their top management was very dubious—a ferroalloy plant to be located in the very poorest area where almost everybody was unemployed. It would create 1,500 jobs in a dying small town of 12,000 people and another 800 jobs for unemployed coal miners—clean, healthy, safe jobs, since the new diggings would be strip mines.

But the plant would have to use an already obsolete high-cost process, the only one for which raw materials were locally available. It would therefore be marginal in both costs and product quality. Also the process was a singularly dirty one, and putting in the best available pollution controls would make it even less economical. Yet it was the only plant that could possibly be put in the neediest area. What did I think?

I said, "Forget it"—which was, of course, not what the three young men wanted to hear and not the advice they followed.

This, as some readers have undoubtedly recognized, is the pre-history of what has become a notorious "environmental crime," the Union Carbide plant in Marietta, Ohio. When first opened in 1951, the plant was an "environmental pioneer." Its scrubbers captured three quarters of the particles spewed out by the smelting furnaces; the standard at the time was half of that or less. Its smokestacks suppressed more fly ash than those of any other power plant then built, and so on.

But within ten years the plant had become an unbearable polluter to Vienna, West Virginia, the small town across the river whose unemployment it was built to relieve. And for five years thereafter the town and Union Carbide fought like wildcats. In the end Union Carbide lost. But while finally accepting federal and state orders to clean up an extremely dirty process, it also announced that it would have to lay off half the 1,500 men now working in the plant—and that's half the people employed in Vienna. The switch to cleaner coal (not to mention the abandonment of strip mining) would also put an end to the 800 or so coal-mining jobs in the poverty hollows of the back country.

There are scores of Viennas around the nation, where marginal plants are kept running precisely because they are the main or only employer in a depressed or decaying area. Should an uneconomical plant shut down, dumping its workers on the welfare rolls? Should the plant be subsidized (which would clearly open the way for everybody to put his hand in the public till)? Should environmental standards be disregarded or their application postponed in "hardship" cases?

If concern for the environment comes to be seen as an attack on the livelihood of workers, public sympathy and political support for it is likely to vanish. It is not too fanciful to anticipate, only a few years hence, the New (if aging) Left, the concerned kids on the campus, and the ministers in a protest march against "ecology" and in support of "the victims of bourgeois environmentalism."

## Third World Ecology

In the poor, developing countries where men must struggle to make even a little progress in their fight against misery, any industry bears a heavy burden of high costs and low productivity. Burdening it further with the cost of environmental control might destroy it. Moreover, development in these countries—regardless of their political creed or social organization, in Mao's as well as in Chiang Kai-shek's China and in North as well as in South Vietnam—cannot occur without the four biggest ecological villains: a rapid increase in electric power, chemical fertilizers and pesticides, the automobile, and the large steel mill.

That poor countries regard those villains as economic saviours confronts us with hard political choices. Should we help such countries get what they want (industrialization), or what we think the world needs (less pollution)? How do we avoid the charge, in either case, that our help is "imperialistic"? To complicate matters, there is a looming conflict between environmental concern and national sovereignty. The environment knows no national boundaries. Just as the smog of England befouls the air of Norway, so the chemical wastes of the French potash mines in Alsace destroy the fish of the lower Rhine in Belgium and Holland.

No matter what the statistics bandied about today, the United States is not the world's foremost polluter. Japan holds this dubious honor by a good margin. No American city can truly compete in air pollution with Tokyo, Milan, Budapest, Moscow, or Düsseldorf. No American river is as much of an open sewer as the lower Rhine, the Seine, or the rivers of the industrial Ukraine such as the lower Dnieper. And we are sheer amateurs in littering highways compared to the Italians, Danes, Germans, French, Swedes, Swiss, and Austrians—although the Japanese, especially in littering mountainsides and camp grounds, are clearly even more "advanced."

If not the worst polluter, however, the United States is clearly the largest one. More important, as the most affluent, most advanced, and biggest of the industrial countries, it is expected to set an example. If we do not launch the environmental crusade, no one else will.

We shall have to make sure, however, that other nations join with us. In the absence of international treaties and regulations, some countries—especially those with protectionist traditions, such as Japan, France, and even the United States—may be tempted to impose ecological standards on imports more severe than those they demand of their own producers. On the other hand, countries heavily dependent on exports, especially in Africa and Latin America, may try to gain a competitive advantage by lax enforcement of environmental standards.

One solution might be action by the United Nations to fix uniform rules obliging all its members to protect the environment: and such action is, in fact, now under official study. The United States might help by changing its import regulations to keep out goods produced by flagrant polluters—allowing ample time for countries with severe poverty and unemployment problems to get the cleanup under way. We have good precedent for such an approach in our own history. Forty years ago we halted the evils of child labor by forbidding the transportation in interstate commerce of goods produced by children.

Such a course, however, will demand extraordinary judgment. Unless we persuade other nations to join with us—and set an example ourselves—we may well be accused of trying again to "police the world."

## Choosing the Lesser Evils

The hardest decisions ahead are even more unprecedented than those we have been discussing. What risks can we afford to take with the environment, and what risks can we *not* afford to take? What are the feasible trade-offs between man's various needs for survival?

Today, for example, no safe pesticides exist, nor are any in sight. We may ban DDT, but all the substitutes so far developed have highly undesirable properties. Yet if we try to do without pesticides altogether, we shall invite massive hazards of disease and starvation the world over. In Ceylon, where malaria was once endemic, it was almost wiped out by large-scale use of DDT: but in only a few years since spraying was halted, the country has suffered an almost explosive resurgence of the disease. In other tropical countries, warns the UN Food and Agricultural Organization, children are threatened with famine because of insect and blight damage to crops resulting from restrictions on spraying. Similarly, anyone who has lately traveled the New England Turnpike will have noticed whole forests defoliated by the gypsy moth, now that we have stopped aerial spraying.

What is the right trade-off between the health hazard to some women taking the pill and the risk of death to others from abortions? How do we balance the thermal and radiation dangers of nuclear power plants against the need for more electricity to fight other kinds of pollution? How should we choose between growing more food for the world's fast-multiplying millions and the banning of fertilizers that pollute streams, lakes, and oceans?

Such decisions should not be demanded of human beings. None of the great religions offers guidance. Neither do the modern "isms," from Maoism to the anarchism popular with the young. The ecological crisis forces man to play God. Despite the fact that we are unequal to the task, we can't avoid it: the risks inherent in refusing to tackle these problems are the greatest of all. We have to try, somehow, to choose some combination of lesser evils; doing nothing invites even greater catastrophe.

## Where to Start

Cleaning up the environment requires determined, sustained effort with clear targets and deadlines. It requires, above all, concentration of effort. Up to now we have had almost complete diffusion. We have tried to do a little bit of everything—and tried to do it in the headlines—when what we ought to do first is draw up a list of priorities in their proper order.

First on such a list belong a few small but clearly definable and highly visible tasks that can be done fairly fast without tying up important resources. Removing the hazard of lead poisoning in old slum tenements might be such an action priority. What to do is well known: burn off the old paint. A substantial number of underemployed black adolescents could be easily recruited to do it.

Once visible successes have been achieved, the real task of priority-setting begins. Then one asks: (1) What are the biggest problems that we know how to solve, and (2) what are the really big ones that we don't know how to solve yet? Clean air should probably head the first list. It's a worldwide problem, and getting worse. We don't know all the answers, but we do have the technological competence to handle most of the problems of foul air today. Within ten years we should have real results to show for our efforts.

Within ten years, too, we should get major results in cleaning up the water around big industrial cities and we should have slowed (if not stopped) the massive pollution of the oceans, especially in the waters near our coastal cities.

As for research priorities, I suggest that the first is to develop birth-control methods that are cheaper, more effective, and more acceptable to people of all cultures than anything we now have. Secondly, we need to learn how to produce electric energy without thermal pollution. A third priority is to devise ways of raising crops for a rapidly growing world population without at the same time doing irreversible ecological damage through pesticides, herbicides, and chemical fertilizers.

Until we get the answers, I think we had better keep on building power plants and growing food with the help of fertilizers and such insect-controlling chemicals as we now have. The risks are well known, thanks to the environmentalists. If they had not created a widespread public awareness of the ecological crisis, we wouldn't stand a chance. But such awareness by itself is not enough. Flaming manifestos and prophecies of doom are no longer much help, and a search for scapegoats can only make matters worse.

What we now need is a coherent, long-range program of action and education of the public and our lawmakers about the steps necessary to carry it out. We must recognize—and we need the help of environmentalists in this task—that we can't do everything at once: that painful choices have to be made, as soon as possible, about what we should tackle first; and that every decision is going to involve high risks and costs, in money and in human lives. Often these will have to be decisions of conscience as well as economics. Is it better, for example, to risk famine or to risk global pollution of earth and water? Any course we adopt will involve a good deal of experimentation—and that means there will be some failures. Any course also will demand sacrifices, often from those least able to bear them: the poor, the unskilled, and the underdeveloped countries. To succeed, the environmental crusade needs support from all major groups in our society, and the mobilization of all our resources, material and intellectual, for years of hard, slow, and often discouraging effort. Otherwise it will not only fail: it will, in the process, splinter domestic and international societies into warring factions.

Now that they have succeeded in awakening us to our ecological peril, I hope the environmentalists will turn their energies to the second and harder task: educating the public to accept the choices we must face, and to sustain a worldwide effort to carry through on the resulting decisions. The time for sensations and manifestos is about over: now we need rigorous analysis, united effort, and very hard work.

# CHAPTER THREE

# Business and Technology

TECHNOLOGY HAS BEEN FRONT-PAGE NEWS for well over a century—and never more so than today. But for all the talk about technology, not much effort has been made to understand it or to study it, let alone to manage it. Economists, historians, and sociologists all stress the importance of technology—but then they tend to treat it with "benign neglect," if not with outright contempt. (On this, see the "Historical Note" at the end of this essay.)

More surprisingly, business and businessmen have done amazingly little to understand technology and even less to manage it. Modern business is, to a very considerable extent, the creature of technology. Certainly the large business organization is primarily the business response to technological development. Modern industry was born when the new technology of power generation—primarily water power at first—forced manufacturing activities out of home and workshop and under the one roof of the modern "factory," beginning with the textile industry in eighteenth-century Britain. And the large business enterprise of today has its roots in the first "big business," the large

---

First published in *Labor, Technology and Productivity*, edited by Jules Backman (New York: New York University Press, 1974).

railroad of the mid-nineteenth century, that is, in technological innovation. Since then, the "growth industries," down to computer and pharmaceutical companies of today, have largely been the out-growth of new technology.

At the same time, business has increasingly become the creator of technology. Increasingly, technological innovation comes out of the industrial laboratory and is being made effective through and in business enterprise. Increasingly, technology depends on business enterprise to become "innovation"—that is, effective action in economy and society.

Yet business managers, or at least a very sizable majority of them, still look upon technology as something inherently "unpredictable." Organizationally and managerially, technological activity still tends to be separated from the main work of the business and organized as a discrete and quite different "R & D" activity which, while in the business, is not really of the business. And until recently business managers, as a rule, did not see themselves as the guardians of technology and as concerned at all with its impact and consequence.

That this is no longer adequate should be clear to every business manager. It is indeed the thesis of this essay that business managers have to learn that technology is managerial opportunity and mana-gerial responsibility. This means specifically:

1. Technology is no more mysterious or "unpredictable" than developments in the economy or society. It is capable of rational anticipation and demands rational anticipation. Business manag-ers have to understand the dynamics of technology. At the very least, they have to understand where technological change is likely to have major economic impact and how to convert tech-nological change into economic results.

2. Technology is not separate from the business and cannot be managed as such if it is to be managed at all. Whatever role "R & D" departments or research laboratories play, the entire business has to be organized as an innovative organization and

has to be capable of technological (but also of social and economic) innovation and change. This requires major changes in structure, in policies, and in attitude.

3. The business manager needs to be concerned as much with the impacts and consequences of technology on the individual, society, and economy as with any other impacts and consequences of his actions. This is not talking "social responsibility"—that is, responsibility for what goes on in society (e.g., minority problems). This is responsibility for impact of one's own actions. And one is always responsible for one's impact.

These last ten years there has been a widely reported "disenchantment with technology." It is by no means the first one in recent history (indeed, similar "disenchantments" have occurred regularly every fifty years or so since the mid-eighteenth century). What is certain, however, is that technology will be more important in the last decades of this century and will, in addition, change more than in the decades just past. Such great needs as the energy crisis, the environmental crisis, and the problems of modern urban society make this absolutely certain. Indeed, one can anticipate, with high probability, that the next twenty-five years will see as much, and as rapid, technological change as did the "heroic age" of invention, the sixty years between the mid-nineteenth century and the outbreak of World War I. In that period, which began in 1856 with Perkin's discovery of aniline dyes and Siemens' design of the first workable dynamo, and which ended in 1911 with the invention of the vacuum tube and with it of modern electronics, today's "modern"—and even tomorrow's "postmodern"—worlds were born. In this "heroic age" a new major invention appeared on the average every fifteen to eighteen months, to be followed almost immediately by the emergence of a new industry based on it. The next twenty-five or thirty years, in all likelihood, will far more resemble this late nineteenth-century period than the fifty years after World War I, which, technologically speaking, were years of refinement and modification rather than of invention. To the business and the businessmen who persist in the traditional attitude toward technology, the attitude which sees in it something "mysterious," something "outside," and something for which other people are responsible, technology will therefore be a deadly threat. But to business and businessmen who accept that technology is *their* tool, but also their responsibility, technology will be a major opportunity.

## Anticipating and Planning Technology

The "unpredictability of technology" is an old slogan. Indeed, it underlies to a considerable extent the widespread "fear of technology." But it is not even true that *invention* is incapable of being anticipated and planned. Indeed, what made the "great inventors" of the nineteenth century—Edison, Siemens, or the Wright brothers—"great" was precisely that they knew how to anticipate technology, to define what was needed and would be likely to have real impact, and to plan technological activity for the specific breakthrough that would have the greatest technological impact—and, as a result, the greatest economic impact.

It is even more true in respect to "innovation" that we can anticipate and plan; indeed, with respect to "innovation," we have to anticipate and plan to have any effect. And it is, of course, with "innovation" rather than with "invention" that the businessman is concerned. Innovation is not a technical, but a social and economic, term. It is a change in the wealth-producing capacity of resources through new ways of doing things. It is not identical with "invention," although it will often follow from it. It is the impact on economic capacity, the capacity to produce and to utilize resources, with which "innovation" is concerned. And this is the area in which business is engaged.

It should be said that technology is no more "predictable" than anything else. In fact, predictions of technology are, at best, useless and are likely to be totally misleading. Jules Verne, the French science fiction writer of a hundred years ago, is remembered today because his predictions have turned out to be amazingly prophetic. What is forgotten is that Jules Verne was only one of several hundred science fiction writers of the late nineteenth century—which indeed was far more the age of science fiction writing than even the present decade. And the other 299 science fiction writers of the time, whose popularity often rivaled and sometimes exceeded that of Jules Verne, were all completely wrong. More important, however, no one could have done anything at the time with Jules Verne's predictions. For most of them, the scientific foundations needed to create the predicted technology did not exist at the time and would not come into being for many years ahead.

For the businessman—but also for the economist or politician—what matters is not "prediction," but the capacity to act. And this cannot be based on "prediction."

But technology can be anticipated. It is not too difficult—though not easy—to analyze existing businesses, existing industries, existing economies and markets to find where a change in technology is needed and is likely to prove economically effective. It is somewhat less easy, though still well within human limitations, to think through the areas in which there exists high potential for new and effective technology.

We can say flatly first that wherever an industry enjoys high and rising demand, without being able to show corresponding profitability, there is need for major technological change and opportunity for it. Such an industry can be assumed, almost axiomatically, to have inadequate, uneconomic, or plainly inappropriate technology. Examples of such industries would be the steel industry in the developed countries since World War II or the paper industry. These are industries in which fairly minor changes in process, that is, fairly minor changes in technology, can be expected to produce major changes in the economics of the industry. Therefore, these are the industries which can become "technology prone." The process either is economically deficient or it is technically deficient—and sometimes both.

We can similarly find "vulnerabilities" and "restraints" which provide opportunities for new technology in the economics of a business and in market and market structure. The questions: what are the demands of customer and market which the present business and the present technology do not adequately satisfy?, and: What are the unsatisfied demands of customer and market?— that is, the basic questions underlying market planning—are also the basic questions to define what technologies are needed, appropriate, and likely to produce economic results with minimum effort.

A particularly fruitful way to identify areas in which technological innovations might be both accessible and highly productive is to ask: "What are we afraid of in this business and in this industry? What are the things which all assert 'can never happen,' but which we nonetheless know perfectly well might happen and could then threaten us? Where, in other words, do we ourselves know at the bottom of our hearts that our products, our technology, our whole approach to the satisfaction we provide to market and customer, is not truly appropriate and no longer completely serves its function?" The typical response of a business to these questions is to deny that they have validity. It is the responsibility of the manager who wants to manage technology for the benefit of his business and of his society to overcome this almost reflexive response and to force himself and his business to take these questions seriously. What is needed is not always new technology. It might equally be a shift to new markets or to new distributive channels. But unless the question is asked, technological opportunities will be missed, will indeed be misconceived as "threats."

These approaches, of which only the barest sketch can be given in this essay, apply just as well to needs of the society as to needs of the market. It is, after all, the function of the businessman to convert need, whether of individual consumer or of the community, into opportunities for business. It is for the identification and satisfaction of that need that business and businessmen get paid. Today's major problems, whether of the city, of the environment, or energy, are similarly opportunities for new technology and for converting existing technology into effective economic action. At the same time, businessmen in managing technology also have to start out from the needs of their own business for new products, new processes, new services to replace what is rapidly becoming old and obsolescent, that is, to replace today. To identify technological needs and technological opportunities one also starts out, therefore, with the assumption that whatever one's business is doing today is likely to be obsolete fairly soon.

This approach assumes a limited and fairly short life for whatever present products, present processes, and present technologies are being applied. It then establishes a "gap," that is, the sales volume which products and processes not yet in existence will have to fill in two, five, or ten years. It thus identifies the scope and extent of technological effort needed. But it also establishes what kind of effort is needed. For it determines why present products and processes are likely to become obsolescent, and it establishes the specifications for their replacement.

Finally, to be able to anticipate technology, to identify what is needed and what is possible, and above all what is likely to be productive technology, the business manager needs to understand the dynamics of technology. It is simply not true that technology is "mysterious." It follows fairly regular and fairly predictable trends. It is not, as is often said, "science." It is not even the "application of science." But it does begin with new knowledge which is then, in a fairly well-understood process, converted into effective—that is, economically productive—application.

## The Pace of Technology

It is often asserted today that technology is moving at a lightning pace, as compared with earlier times. There is no evidence for this assertion. It is equally asserted that new knowledge is being converted much faster into new technology than at any earlier time. This is demonstrably untrue. In fact, there is a good deal of evidence that it takes longer today to convert new knowledge, and especially new scientific knowledge, than it did in the nineteenth century—if not, indeed, in the eighteenth and earlier centuries. There is a lead time, and it is fairly long.

It took some twenty-odd years from Siemens' design of the first effective dynamo to Edison's development of the electric light bulb, which first made possible an electrical industry. It has taken at least as long, in fact it has taken longer, from the design of the first working computer in the early forties to the production of truly effective computers—let alone to the development of the "software" without which a computer is (as was the early electric company) a "cost center" rather than a producer of wealth and economic assets. And there are countless similar examples. The lead time for the conversion of new knowledge into effective technology varies greatly between industries. It is perhaps shortest in the pharmaceutical industry. But even there, it is closer to ten years than to ten months. And, in any one industry, the lead time seems to be fairly constant.

What has shortened is the time between the introduction of new technology into the market and its general acceptance. There is less time to establish a pioneering position, let alone a leadership position. But even there, the "lead time" has not shortened as dramatically as most people, including most businessmen, assume. For both the electric light bulb and the telephone, that is, for the 1880s, the lead time between a successful technological invention and widespread—indeed, worldwide—acceptance was a few months. Within five years after Edison had shown his light bulb to the invited journalists, every one of the major electrical manufacturing companies in existence today in the Western world (excepting only Phillips in Holland) was established, in business, and a leader in its respective market. And the same held true for the telephone and for telephone equipment.

In other words, it is the job of the businessman to understand what new knowledge is becoming acceptable and available, to assess its possible technological impact, and to go to work on converting it into technology—that is, into processes and products. He has to know, for this, not only the science and technology of his own field. Above all, he has to know that major technological "breakthroughs" very often, if not usually, originate in a field of science or knowledge that is different from that in which the old technology had its knowledge foundations. In this sense, the typical approach to "research," that is, the approach of developing specialized expertise in the field in which one already is active, is likely to be a bar to technological leadership rather than its main pillar, as is commonly believed. What is needed, in other words, is a "technologist," rather than a "scientist." And often a layman, with good "feel" for science and technology, and with genuine intellectual interest, does this much better than the highly trained specialist in a technical or a scientific field—who is likely to become the prisoner of his own advanced knowledge.

It is not necessary, it is indeed not even desirable, for the businessman to become a "scientist" or even a "technologist." His role is to be the manager of technology. This requires an understanding of the process of technology and of its dynamics. It requires willingness to anticipate tomorrow's technology and, above all, willingness to accept that today's technology with its processes and products is becoming obsolete rapidly. It requires identifying the needs for new technology and the opportunities for it, in the vulnerabilities and restraints of the business, in the needs of the market and in the needs of society. Above all, it requires acceptance of the fact that technology has to be considered a major business opportunity, the identification and exploitation of which is what the businessman is paid for.

## The Innovative Organization

The next quarter century, as has already been said, is likely to require innovation and technological change as great as any we have ever witnessed. Most of this, however, in sharp contrast to the nineteenth century, will have to be done in and by established organizations, and especially in and by established businesses.

It is not true, as is often said, that "big business monopolizes innovation." On the contrary, the last twenty-five years have been preeminently years in which small business and often new and totally unknown businesses produced a very large share of the most effective innovations. Xerox was nothing but a small paper merchant as late as 1950. Even IBM was still a small company and a mere pygmy, even in its own office equipment industry, as late as World War II. Most of today's pharmaceutical giants were either small companies at the end of World War II or barely in existence, and so on.

But still, increasingly, the major effort in technological change is in development and in market introduction. These do not require "genius." They require very large numbers of competent people and large sums of capital. Both are indeed found in established institutions, whether business or government.

Altogether the existing businesses will have to become innovative organizations. For the last fifty to seventy-five years our emphasis has, properly, been on managing what we already know and understand. For the pace of technological innovation—and even the pace of economic change—in these last seventy-five years was, contrary to popular belief, singularly slow.

Now business will again have to become entrepreneurial. And the entrepreneurial function, as the first great Continental European economist J. B. Say (1767–1832) saw clearly almost two centuries ago, is to move existing resources from areas of lesser productivity to areas of greater productivity. It is to create wealth not by discovering new continents, but by discovering new and better uses for the existing resources and for the known and already exploited economic potentials. And technology, while not the only tool for this purpose, is an important one and may well be the most important one.

The great task of business can be defined as counteracting the specific "law of entropy" of any economic system: the law of the diminishing productivity of capital. It was on this "law" that Karl Marx based his prediction of the imminent demise of the "bourgeois system." Yet capital has not only not become less productive, it has steadily increased its productivity in the developed countries—contrary to the assumed "law." But Karl Marx was right in his premise. Left to its own devices, any economy will indeed move toward steadily diminishing productivity of capital. The only way to prevent it from becoming entropic, the only way to prevent it from degenerating into sterile rigidity, is the constant renewal of the productivity of capital through entrepreneurship—that is, through moving resources from less productive into more productive employment. This, therefore, makes technology the more important the more highly developed technologically a society and economy become.

In the next twenty-five years, when the world will have to grapple with a population problem, an energy problem, a resources problem, and a problem of the basic community, that is, the city, this function is likely to become increasingly more critical—independent, by the way, of the political, social, or economic structure in a developed economy, that is, independent of whether the "system" is "capitalist," "socialist," "Communist," or something else.

This will require businessmen to learn how to build and how to manage an innovative organization. Normally, the innovative organization is being discussed in terms of "creativity" and of "attitudes." What it requires, however, are policies, practices, and structure. It requires, first, that management anticipate technological needs, identify them, plan for them, and work on satisfying them.

It requires, second, and perhaps more important, that management systematically abandon yesterday.

"Creativity" is largely an excuse for doing nothing. The problem in most organizations which are incapable of innovation and self-renewal is that they cannot slough off the old, the outworn, the no longer productive. On the contrary, they tend to allocate to it their best resources, especially of good people. And any body incapable of eliminating waste products poisons itself eventually. What is needed to make an organization innovative is a systematic policy for abandoning the no longer truly productive, the no longer truly contributing. The innovative organization requires, above all, that every product, every process, every activity, be put "on trial for its life" periodically—maybe every two or three years. The question should be asked: "If we did not do this already, would we now—knowing what we now know—go into it?" And if the answer is No, then one does not ask: "Should we abandon it?" Then one asks: "How can we abandon it, and how fast?"

The organization, whether business, university, or government agency, which systematically sloughs off yesterday, need not worry about "creativity." It will have such a healthy appetite for the new that the main task of management will be to select from among the large number of good ideas for the new the ones with the highest potential of contribution and the highest potential of successful completion.

But beyond this, the innovative organization needs specific policies. It needs measurement and information systems which are appropriate to the economic reality of innovation—and a regular, moderate, and continuous "rate of return on investment" is the wrong measurement. Innovation, by definition, is only cost for many years, before it produces a "profit." It is first an investment—and a return only much later. But that also means that the rate of return must be far larger than the highest "rate of return" for which managers plan in a managerial type of business. Precisely because the lead time is long and the failure rate high, a successful innovation in an innovative organization must aim at creating a new business with its potential for creating wealth, rather than a nice and pleasant addition to what we already have and what we already do.

Finally, we will have to realize that innovative work is not capable of being organized and done within managerial components, that is, units concerned primarily with work on today and on tomorrow morning. It needs to be organized separately, with different structural principles and in different structural components. Above all, the demands on managerial self-discipline and on clarity of direction and objectives are much greater in innovative work and have to be extended to a much larger circle of people. And therefore, the innovative organization, while organically a part of the ongoing business, needs to be structurally and managerially separate. Businessmen, to be able to build and lead innovative organizations, will, therefore, have to be able to do both—manage what is already known and create the new and unknown. They will have to be able to optimize the existing business and to maximize the potential business.

These, to most businessmen, are strange and indeed somewhat frightening ideas. But there are plenty of truly innovative businesses around—in practically every country—to show that the task can be done, and is indeed eminently doable. In fact, what is needed primarily is recognition—lacking so far in most management thinking and in almost all management literature—that the innovative organization is a distinct and different organization, and is not only a slightly modified managerial organization.

## Responsibility for the Impact of Technology

Everybody is responsible for the impact of his actions. This is one of the oldest principles of the law. It applies to technology as well. There is a great deal of talk today about "social responsibility." But surely the first point is not responsibility for what society is doing, but responsibility for what one is doing oneself. And therefore, technology has to be considered under the aspect of the businessman's responsibility for the social impacts of his acts. In particular, there is the question of the "by-product impacts," that is, the impacts which are not part of the specific function of a process or product but are, necessarily or not, occurring without intention, without adding to the intended or wanted contribution, and indeed as an additional cost—for every by-product which is not converted into a "salable product" is, in effect, a waste and therefore a cost.

The topic of the responsibility of business for its social impacts is a very big one. And the impacts of technology, no matter how widely publicized today, are among the lesser impacts. But they can be substantial. Therefore, the businessman has to think through what his responsibilities are and how he can discharge them.

There is, these days, great interest in "technology assessment," that is, in anticipating impacts and side effects of new technology *before* going ahead with it. The U.S. Congress has actually set up an Office of Technology Assessment. This new agency is expected to be able to predict what *new technologies* are likely to become important, and what long-range effects they are likely to have. It is then expected to advise government what new technologies to encourage and what new technologies to discourage, if not to forbid altogether.

This attempt can only end in fiasco. "Technology assessment" of this kind is likely to lead to the encouragement of the wrong technologies and the discouragement of the technologies we need. For *future* impacts of *new* technology are almost always beyond anybody's imagination.

DDT is an example. It was synthesized during World War II to protect American soldiers against disease-carrying insects, especially in the tropics. Some of the scientists then envisaged the use of the new chemical to protect civilian populations as well. But not one of the many men who worked on DDT thought of applying the new pesticide to control insect pests infecting crops, forests, or livestock. If DDT had been restricted to the use for which it was developed, that is, to the protection of human beings, it would never have become an environmental hazard; use for this purpose accounted for no more than 5 or 10 percent of the total at DDT's peak, in the mid-sixties. Farmers and foresters, without much help from the scientists, saw that what killed lice on men would also kill lice on plants, and made DDT into a massive assault on the environment.

Another example is the "population explosion" in the developing countries. DDT and other pesticides were a factor in it. So were the new antibiotics. Yet the two were developed quite independently of each other; and no one "assessing" either technology could have foreseen their convergence—indeed, no one did. But more important as causative factors in the sharp drop in infant mortality, which set off the "population explosion," were two very old "technologies" to which no one paid any attention. One was the elementary public health measure of keeping latrine and well apart—known to the Macedonians before Alexander the Great. The other one was the wire-mesh screen for doors and windows invented by an unknown American around 1860. Both were suddenly adopted even by backward tropical villages after World War II. Together they were probably the main "causes" of the "population explosion."

At the same time, the "technology impacts" which the "experts" predict almost never occur. One example is the "private flying boom," which the experts predicted during and shortly after World War II. The private plane, owner-piloted, would become as common, we were told, as the Model T automobile had become around World War I. Indeed, "experts" among city planners, engineers, and architects advised New York City not to go ahead with the second tube of the Lincoln Tunnel, or with the second deck on the George Washington Bridge, and instead to build a number of small airports along the west bank of the Hudson River. It would have taken fairly elementary mathematics to disprove this particular "technology assessment"—there just is not enough airspace for commuter traffic by air. But this did not occur to any of the "experts": no one then realized how finite airspace is. At the same time, almost no "expert" foresaw the expansion of commercial air traffic at the time the jet plane was first developed or that it would lead to mass transportation by air, with as many people crossing the Atlantic in one jumbo jet twelve times a day as used to go once a week in a big passenger liner. To be sure, transatlantic travel was expected to grow fast—but of course it would go by ship. These were the years in which all the governments along the North Atlantic heavily subsidized the building of new super-luxury liners, just when the passengers deserted the liner and switched to the new jet plane.

A few years later, we were told by everybody that "automation" would have tremendous economic and social impacts—it has had practically none. The computer offers an even odder story. In the late forties, nobody predicted that the computer would be used by business and governments. While the computer was a "major scientific revolution," everybody "knew" that its main use would be in science and warfare. As a result, the most extensive market research study undertaken at that time reached the conclusion that the world computer market would, at most, be able to absorb 1,000 computers by the year 2000. Only twenty years later, there were some 150,000 computers installed in the world, most of them doing the most mundane bookkeeping work.

Then, a few years later, when it became apparent that business was buying computers for payroll or billing, the "experts" predicted that the computer would displace "middle management," so that there would be nobody left between the chief executive officer and the foreman. "Is middle management obsolete?" asked a widely quoted *Harvard Business Review* article in the early fifties; and it answered this rhetorical question with a resounding Yes. At exactly that moment, the tremendous expansion of middle management jobs began. In every developed country middle management jobs, in business as well as in government, have grown about three times as fast as total employment in the last twenty years: and this growth has been parallel to the growth of computer usage.

Anyone depending on "technology assessment" in the early fifties would have abolished the graduate business schools as likely to produce graduates who could not possibly find jobs. Fortunately, the young people did not listen and flocked in record numbers to the graduate business schools so as to get the good jobs which the computer helped to create.

But while no one foresaw the computer impact on middle management jobs, every "expert" predicted a tremendous computer impact on business strategy, business policy, planning, and top management—on none of which the computer has, however, had the slightest impact at all. At the same time, no one predicted the real "revolution" in business policy and strategy in business in the fifties and sixties, the merger wave and the "conglomerates."

## Difficulty of Prediction

It is not only that man no more has the gift of prophecy in respect to technology than in respect to anything else. The impacts of technology are actually more difficult to predict than most other developments. In the first place, as the example of the "population explosion" shows, social and economic impacts are almost always the result of the convergence of a substantial number of factors, not all of them technological. And each of these factors has its own origin, its own development, its own dynamics, and its own experts. The "expert" in one field, e.g., the expert on epidemiology, never thinks of plant pests. The expert on antibiotics is concerned with the treatment of disease—whereas the actual explosion of the birth rate largely resulted from elementary and long-known public health measures.

But, equally important, what technology is likely to become important and have an impact, and what technology either will fizzle out—like the "flying Model T"—or will have minimal social or economic impacts—like "automation"—is impossible to predict. And which technology will have social impacts and which will remain just technology is even harder to predict. The most successful prophet of technology, Jules Verne, predicted a great deal of twentieth-century technology a hundred years ago (though few scientists or technologists of that time took him seriously). Yet he anticipated absolutely no social or economic impacts, but an unchanged mid-Victorian society and economy. Economic and social prophets, in turn, have the most dismal record as predictors of technology.

The one and only effect an "Office of Technology Assessment" is likely to have, therefore, would be to guarantee full employment to a lot of fifth-rate science fiction writers.

## The Need for Technology Monitoring

However, the major danger is that the delusion that we can foresee the "impacts" of new technology will lead us to slight the really important task. For technology does have impacts, and serious ones, beneficial as well as detrimental ones. These do not require prophecy. They require careful monitoring of the actual impact of a technology once it has become effective. In 1948, practically no one correctly saw the impacts of the computer. Five and six years later, one could and did know. Then one could say: "Whatever the technological impact, *socially* and *economically* this is not a major threat." In 1943, no one could predict the impact of DDT. Ten years later, DDT had become a worldwide tool of farmer, forester, and livestock breeder, and, as such, a major ecological factor. Then, thinking as to what action to take should have begun, work should have been started on the development of pesticides without the major environmental impact of DDT, and the difficult "tradeoffs" should have been faced between food production and environmental damage—which neither the unlimited use nor the present complete ban on DDT sufficiently considers.

"Technology monitoring" is a serious, an important, indeed a vital task. But it is not "prophecy." The only thing possible. in respect to *new* technology, is *speculation* with about one chance in a hundred of being right—and a much better chance of doing harm by encouraging the wrong, or discouraging the most beneficial new technology. What needs to be watched is "developing" technology, that is, technology which has already had substantial impacts, enough to be judged, to be measured, to be evaluated.

And "monitoring" a "developing" technology for its social impacts is, above all, a managerial responsibility.

But what should be done once such an impact has been identified? Ideally, it should be eliminated. Ideally, the fewer the impacts, the fewer "costs" are being incurred, whether actual business costs, externalities, or social costs. Ideally, therefore, businesses start out with the commitment to convert the elimination of such an impact into "business opportunity."

And where this can be done, the problem disappears, or rather, it becomes a profitable business and the kind of contribution for which business and businessmen are properly being paid. But where this is not possible, business should have learned, as a result of the last twenty years, that it is the task of business to think through what kind of regulation is appropriate. Sooner or later, the impact becomes unbearable. It does no good to be told by one's public relations people that the "public" does not worry about the impact, that it would, in fact, react negatively toward any attempt to come to grips with it. Sooner or later, there is then a "scandal." The business which has not worked on anticipating the problem and on finding the right solution, that is, the right regulation, will then find itself both stigmatized and penalized—and properly so.

This is not the popular thing to say. The popular thing is to assert that the problems are obvious. They are not. In fact, anyone who would have asked for regulation to cut down on air pollution from electric-power plants twenty or even ten years ago would have been attacked as an "enemy of the consumer" and as someone who, "in the name of profit," wanted to make electricity more expensive.

(Indeed, this was the attitude of regulatory commissions when the problem was brought to their attention by quite a few power companies.) When the Ford Motor Company in the early fifties introduced seat belts, it almost lost the market. And the pharmaceutical companies were soundly trounced by the medical profession every time they timidly pointed out that the new high-potency drugs required somewhat more knowledge of pharmacology, biology, and biochemistry than most practicing physicians could be expected to have at their disposal.

But these examples also, I think, bring out that the "public relations" attitude is totally inappropriate and, in fact, self-defeating. They bring out that neglect of the impacts and willingness to accept that "nobody is worried about it" in the not-so-very-long run penalizes business far more seriously than willingness to be unpopular could possibly have done.

Therefore, in technology-monitoring, the businessman not only has to organize an "early-warning" system to identify impacts, and especially unintended and unforeseen impacts. He then has to go to work to eliminate such impacts. The best way, to repeat, is to make the elimination of these impacts into an opportunity for profitable business. But if this cannot be done, then it is the better part of wisdom to think through the necessary public regulation and to start early the education of public, government, and also of one's own competitors and colleagues in the business community. Otherwise the penalty will be very high—and the technology we need to tackle the central problems of "post-industrial" society will meet with growing resistance.

## Conclusion

Technology is certainly no longer the Cinderella of management, which it has been for so long. But it is still to be decided whether it will become the beautiful and beloved bride of the prince, or instead turn into the fairy tale's wicked stepmother. Which way it will go will depend very largely on the business executive and his ability and willingness to manage technology. But which way it will go will also very largely determine which way business will go. For we need new technology, both major "breakthroughs" and the technologically minor but economically important and productive changes to which the headlines rarely pay attention. If business cannot provide them, business will be replaced as a central institution—and will deserve to be replaced. Managing technology is no longer a separate and subsidiary activity that can be left to the "longhairs" in "R & D." It is a central management task.

## A Historical Note

The absence of any serious concern with, and study of, technology among the major academic disciplines is indeed puzzling. In fact, it is so puzzling as to deserve some documentation.

The nineteenth-century economist usually stressed the central importance of technology. But he did not go beyond paying his elaborate respects to technology. In his system, he relegated technology to the shadowy limbo of "external influences," somewhat like earthquakes, locusts, or wind and weather, and as such incomprehensible, unpredictable, and somehow not quite respectable. Technology could be used to explain away phenomena which did not fit the economist's theoretical model. But it could not be used as part of the model. The twentieth-century Keynesian economist does not even make the formal bow to technology which his nineteenth-century predecessor regarded as appropriate. He simply disregards it. There are, of course, exceptions. Joseph Schumpeter, the great Austro-American economist, in his first and best-known work on the dynamics of economic development, put the "innovator" into the center of his economic system. And the innovator in large part was a technological innovator. But Schumpeter found few successors. Among living economists only Kenneth Boulding at the University of Colorado seems to pay any attention to technology.

The ruling schools, whether Keynesian, Neo-Keynesian, or Fried-manite, pay as little attention to technology as the pre-industrial schools of economists, such as the Mercantilists before Adam Smith. But they have far less excuse for this neglect of technology.

Historians, by and large, have paid even less attention to technology than economists. Technology was more or less considered as not worth the attention of a "humanist." Even economic historians have given very little attention to technology until fairly recently. Interest in technology as a subject of study for the historian did not begin until Lewis Mumford's book *Technics and Civilizations* (New York: Harcourt Brace, 1934). It was not until twenty-five years later that systematic work on the study of the history of technology began, with publication in England in 1954–58 of *A History of Technology*, edited by Charles Singer (London; Oxford University Press, 1954–58), five vols.; and shortly thereafter in the United States with the founding of the Society for the History of Technology in 1958 and of its journal, *Technology and Culture*. The relationship between technology and history has further been discussed in the first American textbook, *Technology in Western Civilization*, edited by Melvin Kranzberg and Carroll W. Pursell, Jr. (New York: Oxford University Press, 1967), 2 vols., and in my essay volume: *Technology, Management & Society* (New York: Harper & Row, 1970) (especially in the essays, "Work and Tools" first published in *Technology and Culture* [Winter 1959], "The Technological Revolution," "Notes on the Relationship of Technology, Science and Culture" first published in *Technology and Culture* [Fall 1961], and "The First Technological Revolution and Its Lessons," delivered as Presidential Address to the Society for the History of Technology in December 1965, and first published in *Technology and Culture* [Spring 1966]). The California medievalist Lynn White, Jr., has done pioneering work on the impact of technological changes on society and economy, especially in his book *Medieval Technology and Social Change* (London: Oxford University Press, 1962). But the only work that tries successfully to integrate technology into history, particularly economic history, is the recent book by the Harvard economic historian David S. Landes, *The Unbound Prometheus: Technological Change and Industrial Development in Western Europe: 1750 to the Present* (London: Cambridge University Press, 1969). Outside of the English-speaking countries, only one historian of rank has given any attention to technology, the German Franz Schnabel in his *Deutsche Geschichte im Neunzehnten Jahrhundert* (Freiburg: Herder, 1929–37).

Perhaps even more perplexing is the attitude of the sociologist. While the word "technology" goes back to the seventeenth century, it first became a widely used term as slogan if not as manifesto of the early sociologists in the late eighteenth century. To call the first technical university in 1794 *Ecole Polytechnique* was, for instance, a clear declaration of the central importance of technology to society and social structure. And the early fathers of sociology, especially the great French sociologists, Saint-Simon and Auguste Comte, did indeed see technology as the great liberating force in society. Marx still echoes some of this—but then relegates technology to the realm of secondary phenomena. Sociologists since then have tended to follow Marx and to put the emphasis on property relationships, kinship relationships, and on everything else, but not on technology. There are plenty of slogans such as that of "alienation." But there has been practically no work done. And technology is barely mentioned in the major sociological theories of the last, that is, the post-Marx, century from Max Weber to Marcuse and Levy-Bruhl to Lévi-Strauss and Talcott Parsons. Technology either does not exist at all for the sociologist, or it is an unspecified "villain."

In other words, the scholars have yet to start work on technology, as the way man works; as the extension of the limited physical equipment of the biological creature that is man; as a part—a major part—of man's intellectual history and intellectual achievement; and as a human achievement which, in turn, influences the human condition profoundly. However, the businessman cannot wait for the scholars. He has to manage technology now.

# CHAPTER FOUR

# Multinationals and Developing Countries

## *Myths and Realities*

I

FOUR ASSUMPTIONS ARE commonly made in the discussion of multinationals and developing countries—by friends and enemies alike of the multinational company. All four of these assumptions are false, which explains in large measure both the acrimony of the debate and the sterility of so many development policies.

These four false but generally accepted assumptions are: (1) The developing countries are important to the multinational companies and a major source of sales, revenues, profits, and growth for them, if not the mainstay of "corporate capitalism"; (2) foreign capital, whether supplied by governments or by businesses, can supply the

First published in *Foreign Affairs: An American Quarterly Review*, October 1974.

resources, and especially the capital resources, required for economic development; (3) the ability of the multinational company to integrate and allocate productive resources on a global basis and across national boundaries, and thus to substitute transnational for national economic considerations, subordinates the best national interests of the developing country to "global exploitation"; (4) the traditional nineteenth-century form of corporate organization, that is, the "parent company" with wholly owned "branches" abroad, is also the right form of organization for the twentieth-century multinational company.


II


What are the realities?

In the first instance, extractive industries have to go wherever the petroleum, copper ore, or bauxite is found, whether in a developing or in a developed country. But for the typical twentieth-century multinational, that is, a manufacturing, distributing, or financial company, developing countries are important neither as markets nor as producers of profits. Indeed it can be said bluntly that the major manufacturing, distributive, and financial companies of the developed world would barely notice it, were the sales in and the profits from the developing countries suddenly to disappear.

Confidential inside data in my possession on about forty-five manufacturers, distributors, and financial institutions among the world's leading multinationals, both North American and European, show that the developed two thirds of Brazil—from Bello Horizonte southward—is an important market for some of these companies, though even Brazil ranks among the first twelve sales territories, or among major revenue producers, for only two of them. But central and southern Brazil, while still "poor," are clearly no longer "underdeveloped." And otherwise not even India or Mexico—the two "developing" countries with the largest markets—ranks for any of the multinational companies in my sample ahead even of a single major sales district in the home country, be it the Hamburg-North Germany district, the English Midlands, or Kansas City.

On the worldwide monthly or quarterly sales and profit chart, which most large companies use as their most common top management tool, practically no developing country even appears in my sample of forty-five major multinationals except as part of a "region," e.g., "Latin America," or "Others."

The profitability of the businesses of these companies in the developing countries is uniformly lower by about 2 percentage points than that of the businesses in the developed countries, except for the pharmaceutical industry, where the rate of return, whether on sales or on invested capital, is roughly the same for both. As a rule, it takes longer—by between eighteen months and three years—to make a new operation break even in a developing country. And the growth rate—again excepting the pharmaceutical industry—is distinctly slower. Indeed, in these representative forty-five businesses, 75 to 85 percent of all growth, whether in sales or in profits, in the last twenty-five years, occurred in the developed countries. In constant dollars, the business of these forty-five companies in the developed world doubled—or more than doubled—in the last ten to fifteen years. But their business in the developing countries grew by no more than one third during that period if the figures are adjusted for inflation.

Published data, while still scarce and inadequate, show the same facts. Only for the extractive industries have the developing countries—and then only a very few of them—been of any significance, whether as a source of profits, as loci of growth, or as areas of investment.

The reason is, of course, that—contrary to the old, and again fashionable, theory of "capitalist imperialism"—sales, growth, and profits are where the market and the purchasing power are.

To the developing country, however, the multinational is both highly important and highly visible.

A plant employing 750 people and selling eight million dollars worth of goods is in most developing countries a major employer—both of rank and file and of management—and a big business. For the multinational parent company, employing altogether 97,000 people and selling close to two billion dollars worth of goods a year, that plant is, however, at best marginal. Top management in Rotterdam, Munich, London, or Chicago can spend practically no time on it.

Neglect and indifference rather than "exploitation" is the justified grievance of the developing countries in respect to the multinationals. Indeed, top management people in major multinationals who are personally interested in the developing countries find themselves constantly being criticized for neglecting the important areas and for devoting too much of their time and attention to "outside interests." Given the realities of the business, its markets, growth opportunities, and profit opportunities, this is a valid criticism.

The discrepancy between the relative insignificance of the affiliate in a developing country and its importance and visibility for the host country poses, however, a major problem for the multinationals as well. Within the developing country, the man in charge of a business with 750 employees and eight million dollars in sales has to be an important man. While his business is minute compared to the company's business in Germany, Great Britain, or the United States, it is every whit as difficult—indeed, it is likely to be a good deal more difficult, risky, and demanding. And he has to treat as an equal with the government leaders, the bankers, and the business leaders of his country—people whom the district sales manager in Hamburg, Rotterdam, or Kansas City never even sees. Yet his sales and profits are less than those of the Hamburg, Rotterdam, or Kansas City sales district. And his growth potential is, in most cases, even lower.

This clash between two realities—the personal qualifications and competence, the position, prestige, and power needed by the affiliate's top management people to do their job in the developing country, and the reality of a "sales district" in absolute, quantitative terms—the traditional corporate structure of the multinationals cannot resolve.

III

The second major assumption underlying the discussion of multinationals and developing countries is the belief that resources from abroad, and especially capital from abroad, can "develop" a country.

But in the first place no country is "underdeveloped" because it lacks resources. "Underdevelopment" is inability to obtain full performance from resources; indeed, we should really be talking of countries of higher and lower productivity rather than of "developed" or "underdeveloped" countries. In particular, very few countries—Tibet and New Guinea may be exceptions—lack *capital*. Developing countries have, almost by definition, more capital than they productively employ. What "developing" countries lack is the full ability to mobilize their resources, whether human resources, capital, or the physical resources. What they need are "triggers," stimuli from abroad and from the more highly developed countries, that will energize the resources of the country and will have a "multiplier impact."

The two success stories of development in the last hundred years—Japan and Canada—show this clearly. In the beginning, Japan imported practically no capital except small sums for early infrastructure investments, such as the first few miles of railroad. It organized, however, quite early, what is probably to this day the most efficient system for gathering and putting to use every drop of capital in the country. And it imported—lavishly and without restraints—technology with a very high multiplier impact, and has continued to do so to this day.

Canada, in the mid-1930s, was far less "developed" a country than most Latin-American republics are today. Then the liberal government of the 1930s decided to build an effective system for collecting domestic capital and to put it into infrastructure investments with a very high "multiplier" effect—roads, health care, ports, education, and effective national and provincial administrations. Foreign capital was deliberately channeled into manufacturing and mining. Domestic capital and entrepreneurs were actually discouraged in the extractive and manufacturing sectors. But they were strongly encouraged in all tertiary activities such as distribution, banking, insurance, and in local supply and finishing work in manufacturing. As a result, a comparatively small supply of foreign capital—between a tenth and a twentieth of Canada's total capital formation—led to very rapid development within less than two decades.

There is a second fallacy in the conventional assumption, namely, that there is unlimited absorptive capacity for money and especially for money from abroad. But in most developing countries there are actually very few big investment opportunities. There may be big hydroelectric potential; but unless there are customers with purchasing power, or industrial users nearby, there is no economic basis for a power plant. Furthermore, there is no money without strings. To service foreign capital, even at a minimal interest rate, requires foreign exchange. At that, loans or equity investments as a rule constitute a smaller (and, above all, a clearly delimited) burden than grants and other political subsidies from abroad. The latter always create heavy obligations in terms of both foreign and domestic policy, no matter where they come from.

A developing country will therefore get the most out of resources available abroad, especially capital, if it channels capital where it has the greatest "multiplier impact." Moreover, it should channel it where one dollar of imported capital will generate the largest number of domestic dollars in investment, both in the original investment itself and in impact-investment (e.g., the gas stations, motels, and auto repair shops which an automobile plant calls into being), and where one job created by the original investment generates the most jobs directly and indirectly (again an automobile industry is a good example). Above all, the investment should be channeled where it will produce the largest number of local managers and entrepreneurs and generate the most managerial and entrepreneurial competence. For making resources fully effective depends on the supply and competence of the managerial and entrepreneurial resource.

According to all figures, government money has a much lower multiplier impact than private money. This is, of course, most apparent in the Communist-bloc countries; low, very low, productivity of capital is the major weakness of the Communist economies, whether that of Russia or of its European satellites. But it is true also of public (e.g., World Bank) money elsewhere: it generates little, if any, additional investment either from within or from without the recipient country. And "prestige" investments, such as a steel mill, tend to have a fairly low multiplier impact—both in jobs and in managerial vigor—as against, for instance, a department store which brings into existence any number of small local manufacturers and suppliers and creates a major managerial and entrepreneurial cluster around it.

For the multinational in manufacturing, distribution, or finance locating in a developing country, rapid economic development of the host country offers the best chance for growth and profitability. The multinational thus has a clear self-interest in the "multiplier" impact of its investment, products, and technology. It would be well advised to look on the capital it provides as "pump priming" rather than as "fuel." The more dollars (or pesos or cruzeiros) of local capital each of its own dollars of investment generates, the greater will be the development impact of its investment, and its chance for success. For the developing country the same holds true: to maximize the development impact of each imported dollar is its greatest need.

The Canadian strategy was carried on too long; by the early 1950s, Canada had attained full development and should have shifted to a policy of moving its own domestic capital into "super-structure" investments. But though the Canadian strategy is certainly not applicable to many developing countries today—and though, like any strategy, it was made obsolete by its very success—nevertheless it was highly successful, very cheap, and resulted in rapid economic growth, while at the same time ensuring a high degree of social development and social justice.

What every developing country needs is a strategy which looks upon the available foreign resources, especially of capital, as the "trigger" to set off maximum deployment of a country's own resources and to have the maximum "multiplier effect." Such a strategy sees in the multinational a means to energize domestic potential—and especially to create domestic entrepreneurial and managerial competence—rather than a substitute for domestic resources, domestic efforts, and, even, domestic capital. To make the multinationals effective agents of development in the developing countries therefore requires, above all, a policy of encouraging the domestic private sector, the domestic entrepreneur, and the domestic manager. If they are being discouraged, the resources brought in from abroad will, inevitably, be wasted.

For by themselves multinationals cannot produce development; they can only turn the crank but not push the car. It is as futile and self-defeating to use capital from abroad as a means to frighten and cow the local business community—as the bright young men of the early days of the Alliance for Progress apparently wanted to do—as it is to mobilize the local business community against the "wicked imperialist multinational."

## IV

The multinational, it is said, tends to allocate production according to global economics. This is perfectly correct, though so far very few companies actually have a global strategy. But far from being a threat to the developing country, this is potentially the developing country's one trump card in the world economy. Far from depriving the governments of the developing countries of decision-making power, the global strategy of the multinationals may be the only way these governments can obtain some effective control and bargaining leverage.

Short of attack by a foreign country, the most serious threat to the economic sovereignty of developing countries, and especially of small ones, i.e., of most of them, is the shortage of foreign exchange. It is an absolute bar to freedom of decision. Realizing this, many developing countries, especially in the 1950s and early 1960s, chose a deliberate policy of "import substitution."

By now we have all learned that in the not-so-very-long run this creates equal or worse import-dependence and foreign-exchange problems. Now a variant of "import substitution" has become fashionable: a "domestic-content" policy which requires the foreign company to produce an increasing part of the final product in the country itself. This, predictably, will eventually have the same consequences as the now discredited "import substitution," namely, greater dependence on raw materials, equipment, and supplies from abroad. And in all but the very few countries with already substantial markets (Brazil is perhaps the only one—but then Brazil is not, after all, "developing" any longer in respect to the central and southern two thirds of the country), such a policy must, inevitably, make for a permanently high-cost industry unable to compete and to grow. The policy creates jobs in the very short run, to be sure; but it does so at the expense of the poor and of the country's potential to generate jobs in the future and to grow.

What developing countries need are *both:* foreign-exchange earnings and productive facilities large enough to provide economies of scale and with them substantial employment. This they can obtain only if they can integrate their emerging productive facilities—whether in manufactured goods or in such agricultural products as fruits and wine—with the largest and fastest-growing economy around, i.e., the world market.

But exporting requires market knowledge, marketing facilities, and marketing finance. It also requires political muscle to overcome strongly entrenched protectionist forces, and especially labor unions and farm blocs in the developed countries. Exporting is done most successfully, most easily, and most cheaply if one has an assured "captive" market, at least for part of the production to be sold in the world market. This applies particularly to most of the developing countries, whose home market is too small to be an adequate base for an export-oriented industry.

The multinational's capacity to allocate production across national boundary lines and according to the logic of the world market should thus be a major ally of the developing countries. The more rationally and the more "globally" production is being allocated, the more they stand to gain. A multinational company, by definition, can equalize the cost of capital across national lines (to some considerable extent, at least). It can equalize to a large extent the managerial resource, that is, it can move executives, can train them, etc. The only resource it cannot freely move is labor. And that is precisely the resource in which the developing countries have the advantage.

This advantage is likely to increase. Unless there is a worldwide prolonged depression, labor in the developed countries is going to be increasingly scarce and expensive, if only because of low birth-rates, while a large-scale movement of people from pre-industrial areas into developed countries, such as the mass movement of American blacks to the northern cities or the mass movement of "guest workers" to western Europe, is politically or socially no longer possible.

But unless the multinationals are being used to integrate the productive resources of the developing countries into the productive network of the world economy—and especially into the production and marketing systems of the multinationals themselves—it is unlikely that major export markets for the production of the developing countries will emerge quickly.

Thus, the most advantageous strategy for the developing countries would seem to be to replace—or, at least, to supplement—the policy of "domestic content" by a policy that uses the multinationals' integrating ability to develop large productive facilities with access to markets in the developed world. A good idea might be to encourage investment by multinationals with definite plans—and eventually firm commitments—to produce for export, especially within their own multinational system. As Taiwan and Singapore have demonstrated, it can make much more sense to become the most efficient large supplier worldwide of one model or one component than to be a high-cost small producer of the entire product or line. This would create more jobs and provide the final product at lower prices to the country's own consumers. And it should result in large foreign-exchange earnings.

I would suggest a second integration requirement. That developing countries want to limit the number of foreigners a company brings in is understandable. But the multinational can be expected to do that anyhow as much as possible—moving people around is expensive and presents all sorts of problems and troubles. Far more important would be a requirement by the developing country that the multinational integrate the managerial and professional people it employs in the country within its worldwide management development plans. Most especially it should assign an adequate number of the younger, abler people from its affiliate in the developing country for three to five years to managerial and professional work in one of the developed countries. So far, to my knowledge, this is being done systematically only by some of the major American banks, by Aluminium Corporation of Canada, and by Nestlé. Yet it is people and their competence who propel development; and the most important competence needed is not technical, i.e., what one can learn in a course, but management of people, marketing, and finance, and first-hand knowledge of developed countries.

In sum, from the point of view of the developing countries, the best cross-national use of resources which the multinational is—or should be—capable of may well be the most positive element in the present world economy. A policy of self-sufficiency is not possible even for the best-endowed country today. Development, even of modest proportions, cannot be based on uneconomically small, permanently high-cost facilities, either in manufacturing or in farming. Nor is it likely to occur, let alone rapidly, under the restraint of a continuous balance-of-payments crisis. The integration of the productive capacities and advantages of developing countries into the world economy is the only way out. And the multinational's capacity for productive integration across national boundaries would seem the most promising tool for this.

## V

That 100 percent ownership on the part of the "parent company" is *the* one and only corporate structure for the multinational, while widely believed, has never been true. In so important a country as Japan, it has always been the rather rare exception, with most non-Japanese companies operating through joint ventures. Sears, Roebuck is in partnership throughout Canada with a leading local retail chain, Simpson's. The Chase Manhattan Bank operates in many countries as a minority partner in and with local banks. Adela, the multinational venture-capital firm in Latin America and for many years the most successful of all development institutions in the world, confined itself from its start to minority participation in its ventures; and so on.

But it is true that, historically, 100 percent ownership has been considered the preferred form, and anything else as likely to make unity of action, vision, and strategy rather difficult. Indeed, restriction of the foreign investor to less than 100 percent control or to a minority participation, e.g., in the Andean Pact agreements or in Mexico's legislation regarding foreign investments, is clearly intended as restraint on the foreigner, if not as punitive action.

But increasingly the pendulum is likely to swing the other way. (Indeed, it may not be too far-fetched to anticipate that, a few years hence, "anti-foreign" sentiment may take the form of demanding 100 percent foreign capital investment in the national company in the developing country, and of moving toward outlawing partnerships or joint ventures with local capital as a drain on a country's slender capital resources.) The multinational will find it increasingly to its advantage to structure ownership in a variety of ways, and especially in ways that make it possible for it to gain access to both local capital and local talent.

Capital markets are rapidly becoming "polycentric." The multinationals will have to learn so to structure their businesses as to be able to tap any capital market—whether in the United States, western Europe, Japan, Brazil, Beirut, or wherever. This the monolithic "parent company" with wholly-owned branches is not easily capable of. When companies, for example the West Europeans, raise money abroad, they often prefer financial instruments such as convertible debentures, which their own home capital markets, or the United States, do not particularly like and cannot easily handle. There is also more and more evidence that the capital-raising capacity of a huge multinational, especially for medium-term working capital, can be substantially increased by making major segments of the system capable of financing themselves largely in their own capital markets and with their own investing public and financial institutions.

But capital is also likely to be in short supply for years to come, barring a major global depression. And this might well mean that the multinationals will only be willing and able to invest in small, less profitable and more slowly growing markets, i.e., in developing countries, if these countries supply a major share of the needed capital rather than have the foreign investor put up all of it.

That this is already happening, the example of Japan shows. Lifting restrictions on foreign investment was expected to bring a massive rush of takeover bids and 100 percent foreign-owned ventures.

Instead, it is now increasingly the Western investor, American as well as European, who presses for joint ventures in Japan and expects the Japanese partner to supply the capital while he supplies technology and product knowledge.

Perhaps more important will be the need to structure for other than 100 percent ownership to obtain the needed managerial talent in the developing country. If the affiliate in the developing country is not a "branch" but a separate company, with substantial outside capital investment, the role and position of its executives become manageable. They are then what they have to be, namely, truly "top management," even though in employment and sales their company may still be insignificant within the giant concern.

And if the multinational truly attempts to integrate production across national boundaries, a "top management" of considerable stature becomes even more necessary. For then, the managers of the affiliate in a developing country have to balance both a national business and a global strategy. They have to be "top management" in their own country and handle on the local level highly complex economic, financial, political, and labor relations, as well as play as full members on a worldwide "systems management" team. To do this as a "subordinate" is almost impossible. One has to be an "equal," with one's own truly autonomous command.

VI

Domestically, we long ago learned that "control" has been divorced from "ownership" and, indeed, is rapidly becoming quite independent of "ownership." There is no reason why the same development should not be taking place internationally—and for the same two reasons: (1) "ownership" does not have enough capital to finance the scope of modern large businesses; and (2) management, i.e., "control," has to have professional competence, authority, and standing of its own. Domestically, the divorce of "control" from "ownership" has not undermined "control." On the contrary, it has made managerial control and direction more powerful, more purposeful, more cohesive.

There is no inherent reason why moving away from "100 percent ownership" in developing countries should make impossible maintenance of common cohesion and central control. On the contrary, both because it extends the capital base of the multinational in a period of worldwide capital shortage and because it creates local partners, whether businessmen or government agencies, the divorce between control and direction may well strengthen cohesion, and may indeed even be a prerequisite to a true global strategy.

At the same time such partnership may heighten the development impact of multinational investment by mobilizing domestic capital for productive investment and by speeding up the development of local entrepreneurs and managers.

Admittedly, mixed ownership has serious problems; but they do not seem insurmountable, as the Japanese joint venture proves. It also has advantages; and in a period of worldwide shortage of capital, it is the multinational that would seem to be the main beneficiary. Indeed, one could well argue that developing countries, if they want to attract foreign investment in such a period, may have to *offer* co-investment capital, and that provisions for the participation of local investment in ownership will come to be seen (and predictably to be criticized) as favoring the foreign investor rather than limiting him.

## VII

The multinational, while the most important and most visible innovation of the postwar period in the economic field, is primarily a symptom of a much greater change. It is a response to the emergence of a genuine world economy. This world economy is not an agglomeration of national economies as was the "international economy" of nineteenth-century international trade theory. It is fundamentally autonomous, has its own dynamics, its own demand patterns, its own institutions—and in the Special Drawing Rights (SDR) even its own money and credit system in embryonic form. For the first time in four hundred years—since the end of the sixteenth century, when the word "sovereignty" was first coined—the territorial political unit and the economic unit are no longer congruent.

This, understandably, appears as a threat to national governments. The threat is aggravated by the fact that no one so far has a workable theory of the world economy. As a result, there is today no proven, effective, predictable economic policy: witness the impotence of governments in the face of worldwide inflation.

The multinationals are but a symptom. Suppressing them, predictably, can only aggravate the disease. But to fight the symptoms in lieu of a cure has always been tempting. It is therefore entirely possible that the multinationals will be severely damaged and perhaps even destroyed within the next decades. If so, this will be done by the governments of the multinationals' *home* countries, the United States, Great Britain, Germany, France, Japan, Sweden, Holland, and Switzerland—the countries where 95 percent of the world's multinationals are domiciled and which together account for at least three quarters of the multinationals' business and profits. The developing nations can contribute emotionalism and rhetoric to the decisions, but very little else. They are simply not important enough to the multinationals (or to the world economy) to have a major impact.

But at the same time the emergence of a genuine world economy is the one real hope for most of the developing countries, especially for the great majority which by themselves are too small to be viable as "national economies" under present technologies, present research requirements, present capital requirements, and present transportation and communications facilities. The next twenty years are the years in which they will both most need the multinationals and have the greatest opportunity of benefiting from them. For these will be the years when the developing countries will have to find jobs and incomes for the largest number of new entrants into the labor force in their history while, at the same time, the developed countries will experience a sharp contraction of the number of new entrants into their labor force—a contraction that is already quite far advanced in Japan and in parts of western Europe and will have reached the United States by the late 1970s. And the jobs that the developing countries will need so desperately for the next ten years will to a very large extent require the presence of the multinationals—their investment, their technology, their managerial competence, and above all their marketing and export capabilities.

The best hope for developing countries, both to attain political and cultural nationhood and to obtain the employment opportunities and export earnings they need, is through the integrative power of the world economy. And their tool, if only they are willing to use it, is, above all, the multinational company—precisely because it represents a global economy and cuts across national boundaries.

The multinational, if it survives, will surely look different tomorrow, will have a different structure, and will be "transnational" rather than "multinational." But even the multinational of today is—or at least should be—a most effective means to constructive nationhood for the developing world.

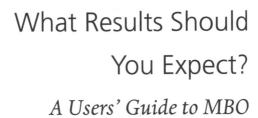

# CHAPTER FIVE

# What Results Should You Expect?

## A Users' Guide to MBO

MANAGEMENT BY OBJECTIVES (MBO) has a longer history in governmental institutions than most of its present-day practitioners realize. The basic concepts were strongly advocated by Luther Gulick and his associates in the mid- and late thirties, in their studies of the organization and administration of the federal government. Yet, the concept of management by objectives and self-control originated with the private sector. It was first practiced by the DuPont Company after World War I. By the mid-twenties, Alfred P. Sloan, Jr., of General Motors used management by objectives and self-control systematically and with great conceptual clarity even though he did not have a special term for his policies.

Yet today MBO seems to have become more popular in public service institutions than it is in the private sector; it is certainly more discussed as a tool of the public, especially the governmental administrator.

First published in *Public Administration Review*, January–February 1976.

There is good reason for this popularity of MBO in the public sector. Public service institutions need it far more than any but the very biggest and most complex businesses. Public service institutions always have multiple objectives and often conflicting, if not incompatible objectives. While no institution, including business, has truly satisfactory measurements, the measurements generally available to government agencies and other public service institutions, especially in the budget area, rarely have anything to do with performance and goal attainment. Even a fairly small governmental agency, such as one of the smaller and less populous States in the U.S. or a medium-sized city, is a "conglomerate" of greater diversity and complexity than the most diversified business "conglomerate."

The resources of public service institutions are people, and the outputs are rarely "things." Therefore, direction toward meaningful results is not inherent in the work or in the process itself. Misdirection, whether by the individual employee or by the administrator, is at the same time both easy and hard to detect. Public service institutions are prone to the deadly disease of "bureaucracy"; that is, toward mistaking rules, regulations, and the smooth functioning of the machinery for accomplishment, and the self-interest of the agency for public service.

Public service institutions, in other words, particularly need objectives and concentration of efforts on goals and results—that is, management. These are, of course, precisely the needs management by objectives and self-control (MBO) promises to satisfy. But the same reasons which make MBO potentially so productive for the public service institution also make it only too easy for the institution to mistake MBO procedures for the substance of both management and objectives. Indeed, they may encourage the fatal error of misusing MBO as a substitute for thinking and decision making.

Therefore, the administrator in the public service institution needs a "users, guide." He needs to know whether he uses MBO correctly or whether he misuses it. He needs to know, above all, the results MBO yields if used properly. That, I am afraid, is what few of the texts and manuals spell out. Yet only when these results have been achieved has MBO really been applied.

MBO is both management by *objectives* and *management* by objectives. What is needed, therefore, are two sets of specifications—one spelling out the results in terms of objectives and one spelling out the results in terms of management.

## What Are Our Objectives? What Should They Be?

The first result, and perhaps the most important one which the administrator needs to aim at in applying MBO, is *the clear realization that his agency actually has no objectives*. What passes for objectives are, as a rule, only good intentions.

The purpose of an objective is to make possible the organization of work for its attainment. This means that objectives must be operational: capable of being converted into specific performance, into work, and into work assignments. However, almost no public service agency has operational objectives. To say our objective is "the maintenance of law and order" or "health care" is operationally a meaningless statement. Nothing can be deduced from these statements with respect to the goals and the work needed. Yet these statements are already a good deal more operational, more nearly true objectives, than is commonly found in the objectives statements of public service agencies.

The first result to be expected from management by *objectives* is the realization that the traditional statement of objectives is inadequate, is indeed in most cases totally inappropriate. The first work to be done is to identify what the objectives should or could be.

The moment this question is raised, however, it will also be realized—and this is the second result to be obtained—that *objectives* in public service agencies are ambiguous, ambivalent, and multiple. (This holds true in private business as well, by the way.)

The hospital, while complex, is still a very small institution compared to most governmental agencies. Yet its objectives are by no means clear. "Health care" sounds plausible; but most hospitals have nothing to do with health care. They are concerned with the treatment and care of the sick. Clearly, the most intelligent and most effective way to produce health care is the prevention of sickness, rather than its treatment and cure. To the extent that we know how to provide health care, it is not, bluntly, the task of the hospital at all. It is done by public health measures such as vaccination, providing pure drinking water, and adequate treatment of sewage. Hospitals, in effect, are the result of the failure of health care, rather than agencies to provide it.

Yet even if the hospital defines its objectives very narrowly, as do the hospitals in the British Health Service, as the "treatment of the sick" (repair of damage already done), the objectives are still cloudy. Is the hospital, as in the traditional concept of the American community hospital, the private physician's plant facility and an extension of his office? Is it, in other words, the place where the physician takes care of those patients whom he cannot take care of in his own office or in his own private practice? Or should the hospital, as so many American hospitals have attempted, be the "health care center" for the community, through such activities as the well-baby clinic, counseling service for the emotionally disturbed, and so on? Should the hospital also become the substitute for the private physician and provide the physician's services to the poor—the objectives of the outpatient department in the American big city hospital today? If the hospital defines its function as care of the sick, what then is the role and function of the maternity service? Giving birth to a baby is, after all, no sickness, but a perfectly normal and indeed perfectly healthy occurrence.

Similarly, when the police department tries to make operational the vague term "maintenance of law and order," it will find immediately that there is a multiplicity of possible objectives—each of them ambiguous. "Prevention of crime" sounds very specific. But what does it really mean, assuming that anyone knows how to do it? Is it, as many police departments have traditionally asserted, the enforcement of all the laws on the statute book? Or is it the protection of the innocent, law-abiding citizen, with respect both to his person and to his property? Is it safety on the streets or safety in the home, or is it both? Is the primary task the eradication and prevention of corruption within the police force itself? The latter may sound quite peripheral, if not trivial. Yet, in a recent major study of the job of chief of police, sponsored by one of the agencies of the Federal government, the experienced police chiefs guiding the study maintained that to rid police forces of corruption was the first, and most important, objective in maintaining law and order.

In attempting to reduce pious intentions to genuine objectives, the administrator will invariably find that equally valid objectives are mutually incompatible or, at least, quite inconsistent.

The classical example is the American farm policy of the last forty years. Strengthening the American farmer was the stated objective from the beginning, before New Deal days. Does this mean protecting the family farmer? Or does it mean making the American farmer efficient, productive, and capable of world market competition? Congress, in writing farm legislation, has always used rhetoric indicating that the purpose of farm policy is to protect and preserve the small family farmer. However, the actual measures then enacted to achieve this purpose have primarily been aimed at making farming a more efficient, more productive, and more competitive industry, in which the small family farmer has practically no place and may indeed be an impediment to the attainment of the goal.

Thus the most important result of management by *objectives* is that it forces the administrator into the realization that there cannot be one single objective, notwithstanding the language of policy statements, whether acts of Congress or administrative declarations. To call realization of this fundamental problem a result of management by *objectives* may seem paradoxical. Yet it may be the most important result, precisely because it forces the administrator and his agency to a realization of the need to think and of the need to make highly risky balancing and trade-off decisions. This should be one of the results management by *objectives* strives for, which have to be attained if MBO is to be an effective tool that strengthens the performance of the institution.

The next area in which management by *objectives* has to attain results is that of *priorities* and *posteriorities*.

Public service institutions, almost without exception, have to strive to attain multiple objectives. At the same time, each area of objectives will require a number of separate goals. Yet no institution, least of all a large one, is capable of doing many things, let alone of doing many things well. Institutions must concentrate and set priorities. By the same token, they must make risky decisions about what to postpone and what to abandon—to think through posteriorities.

One basic reason for this need to concentrate is the communications problem, both within the institution and among the various external publics. Institutions which try to attain simultaneously a great many different goals end up confusing their own members. The confusion is extended twofold to the outside public on whose support they depend.

Another cogent reason for concentration of goals is that no institution has an abundance of truly effective resources. We have all learned that money alone does not produce results. Results require the hard work and efforts of dedicated people; such people are always in short supply. Yet nothing destroys the effectiveness of competent individuals more than having their efforts splintered over a number of divergent concerns—there is nothing more frustrating or less productive than to give part-time attention to a major task. To achieve results always requires thorough and consistent attention to the problem by at least one effective man or woman.

Finally, and this may be the most important factor, even a unitary, or a simple goal often requires a choice between very different strategies which cannot be pursued at the same time; one of them has to be given priority, which means that the other one assumes secondary status or is abandoned for an unspecified time.

One example of this dilemma, which is familiar to every experienced administrator, is the educational policy of developing countries. That a trained and schooled population is desirable, and is indeed a prerequisite for social and economic development, would be accepted by practically all students of development. However, should primary emphasis be given to the education of a small, but exceedingly capable, elite? Or should the main drive be on "mass literacy"? Few countries can pursue both goals simultaneously—they must make a choice. If the first course is followed, there is the risk of educating people to be highly skilled and at great expense to the country. The consequences are that the society cannot utilize the expertise it has paid for and cannot provide meaningful jobs for those individuals. The result is then a "brain drain" in which the potentially most productive, most expensive resources of a poor country leave to find opportunities elsewhere for the application of their knowledge.

If the second alternative is being followed, there is the risk of educating large masses of people who are no longer satisfied with traditional employment and traditional subsistence standards of living. These people cannot find the jobs they have been trained for and have been led to expect, simply because institutions capable of employing them do not emerge, and the leadership is missing.

To set priorities is usually fairly simple, or at least seems politically fairly simple. What is difficult, and yet absolutely essential, is the risk-taking and politically dangerous decision as to what the posteriorities should be. Every experienced administrator knows that what one postpones, one really abandons. In fact, it is a sound rule not to postpone but to make the decision not to do something altogether or to give up doing something. For in strategy, timing is of the essence. Nothing is usually less productive than to do ten years later what would have been an excellent and worthwhile program ten years earlier.

If an illustration were needed, the fate of so many of President Johnson's programs would supply it. What made so many of these programs fail is not that they were the wrong programs, or even that they were inadequately supported. They were, in large measure, five or ten years too late. These programs had been postponed, and when the time came to do them, that is, when Congress was willing to consider them after long years of resistance, they were no longer the "right" programs.

In addition, public service institutions find "abandonment of yesterday" even more difficult than businesses. Business, of course, does not like to abandon. The product or service that no longer serves a purpose, no longer produces results, no longer fulfills a major need, is usually also the product or service which the people now at the top have spent the best part of their working lives to create and to make succeed. However, in business enterprise, the market eventually forces management to face up to reality and to abandon yesterday.

The Ford Motor Company held onto the Edsel as long as it could—far longer than economic reality justified. The American public had abandoned the Edsel long before Ford management was willing to accept the verdict. Eventually, however, even a very large, strong, and stubborn company had to accept reality.

No such pressure exists as a rule in the public service institution. Indeed, if we had had ministries of transportation around in 1850 or 1900, we might now have in every country major research projects, funded with billions of dollars, to reeducate the horse. In any public service institution, whether government agency, hospital, school, or university, any activity and any service almost immediately creates its own constituency: in the legislature, the press, or the public. Yet nothing is quite as difficult to do as to maintain the moribund. It requires greater energies, greater effort, and greater abilities to sustain an obsolete program than to make effective the responsive and productive program.

Thus, the public service agency is always in danger of frittering away its best people as well as a great deal of money on activities which no longer produce, no longer contribute, have proven to be incapable of producing, or are simply inappropriate.

Therefore, essential to management by *objectives* in the public service agency is the establishment of priorities. This requires first decisions concerning the areas of concentration.

Equally essential is the systematic appraisal of all services and activities in order to find the *candidates for abandonment*. Indeed, it is wisdom in a public service agency to put each service and activity on trial for its life every three or four years and to ask: "If we had known what we now know at the time we established this service, would we have gotten into it?" If the answer is No, one does not say, "What do we have to do to make it viable again?" One does not even say, "Should we consider getting out of it?" One says, "How fast can we get out?"

Goals of abandonment and schedules to attain these goals are an essential part of management by *objectives*, however unpopular, disagreeable, or difficult to attain they might be. The great danger in large institutions, especially in public service institutions, is to confuse fat with muscle and motion with performance. The only way to prevent this degenerative disease is a systematic procedure for abandoning yesterday, and for setting specific and courageous goals for abandonment.

In this respect, the Budget Reform Act of 1974 may represent the biggest step forward in public administration in many decades, though it still remains to be seen, of course, whether the act will produce results. This act entrusted the General Accounting Office with the duty of appraising existing programs and projects in the federal service based on their suitability, stated objectives, and appropriateness.

But will the Congress that wrote the act be willing to face up to its abandonment implications?

The next results are *specific goals*, with specific *targets*, specific *timetables*, and specific *strategies*. Implicit in this is the *clear definition of the resources* needed to attain these goals, the efforts needed, and primarily the *allocation* of available resources—especially of available manpower. A "plan" is not a plan unless the resources of competent, performing people needed for its attainment have been specifically allocated. Until then, the plan is only a good intention; in reality not even that.

Finally, management by *objectives* needs to define how performance can be *measured*, or at least *judged*.

It is commonly argued that public service institutions aim at intangible results, which defy measurement. This would simply mean that public service institutions are incapable of producing results. Unless results can be appraised objectively, there will be no results. There will only be activity, that is, costs. To produce results, it is necessary to know what results are desirable and determine whether the desired results are actually being achieved.

It is also not true that the activities of public service institutions cannot be measured.

"Missions" are always intangible, whether of business enterprise or of social service institutions. Sears, Roebuck and Company defined its mission in the twenties as being the "buyer for the American Family." This is totally intangible. But the objectives which Sears then set to accomplish this mission (e.g., to develop a range of appliances that most nearly satisfy the largest number of homeowners at the most economical price) was an operational objective from which clear and measurable goals with respect to product line, service, assortment, price, and market penetration could be derived. This in turn made possible both the allocation of efforts and the measurement of performance.

"Saving souls" as the mission of a church is totally intangible. At least, the bookkeeping is not of this world. However, the goal of bringing at least two thirds of the young people of the congregation into the church and its activities is easily measured.

Similarly, "health care" is intangible. But the goals for a maternity ward which state that the number of "surprises" in delivery must not be more than two or three out of every hundred deliveries; the number of postpartum infections of mothers must not exceed one half of 1 percent of all deliveries; and that eight out of ten of all premature babies born live after the seventh month of conception must survive in good health, are not intangible but fairly easy to measure.

To think through the appropriate measurement is in itself a policy decision and therefore highly risky. Measurements, or at least criteria for judgment and appraisal, define what we mean by performance. They largely dictate where the efforts should be spent. They determine whether policy priorities are serious or are merely administrative doubletalk. For this reason it must be emphasized that measurements need to be measurements of performance rather than of efforts. It is not adequate, indeed it is misleading, to use measurements that focus on efficiency of operation, rather than on the services the agency delivers to somebody outside, whether another public service agency or the public. Measurement directs effort and vision. One of the central problems of public service agencies, indeed of all organizations, is the tendency to direct efforts and vision toward the inside, that is, toward efficiencies, rather than toward the purposes on the outside for which every public service institution exists.

With measurements defined, it then becomes possible to organize the *feedback* from results to activities. What results should be expected by what time? In effect, measurements decide what phenomena are results. Identifying the appropriate measurements enables the administrator to move from diagnosis to prognosis. He can now lay down what he expects will happen and take proper action to see whether it actually does happen.

The actual results of action are not predictable. Indeed, if there is one rule for action, and especially for institutional action, it is that the expected results will not be attained. The unexpected is practically certain. But are the unexpected results deleterious? Are they actually more desirable than the results that were expected and planned? Do the deviations from the planned course of events demand a change in strategies, or perhaps a change in goals or priorities? Or are they such that they indicate opportunities that were not seen originally, opportunities that indicate the need to increase efforts and to run with success? These are questions the administrator in the public service agency rarely asks. Unless he builds into the structure of objectives and strategies the organized feedback that will force these questions to his attention, he is likely to disregard the unexpected and to persist in the wrong course of action or to miss major opportunities.

Organized feedback leading to systematic review and continuous revision of objectives, roles, priorities, and allocation of resources must therefore be built into the administrative process. To enable the administrator to do so is a result, and an important result, of management by *objectives*. If it is not obtained, management by *objectives* has not been properly applied.


## What Is Management? What Should It Be?

*Management* by objectives, similarly, has to attain a number of results to be properly applied.

The first result is *understanding*. *Management* by objectives is often described as a way to obtain agreement. But this is gross oversimplification. The decision which MBO identifies and brings into focus: the decisions on objectives and their balance; on goals and strategies; on priorities and abandonment; on efforts and resource allocation; on the appropriate measurements, are far too complex, risky, and uncertain to be made by acclamation. To make them intelligently requires *informed dissent*.

What MBO has to produce as the first *management* result is understanding of the difficulty, complexity, and risk of these decisions. It is understanding that different people, all employed in a common task and familiar with it, define objectives and goals differently, see different priorities, and would prefer very different and incompatible strategies. Only then can the decision be made effectively.

The decisions to be made are also of such complexity and of such importance that the responsible administrator would not want to make them without understanding them. The full complexity of any issue can only be understood on the basis of informed dissent. "Adversary proceedings" are not the best way, as a rule, to make these decisions. Informed dissent is essential where people of good will and substantial knowledge find out how differently they view the same problem, the same mission, the same task, and the same reality. Otherwise, symptoms rather than the underlying problem will be attacked; trivia rather than results will be pursued.

It is almost fifty years since Mary Parker Follett applied the early insights of perception psychology to point out that people in an organization who seem to differ on the answers usually differ on what the right question is. The issues, with which the administrator in the public service institution deals, are of such complexity and have so many dimensions that any one person can be expected to see only one aspect and only one dimension rather than the total configuration.

However, effective action requires an understanding of complexity. It requires an ability to see a problem in all its major dimensions. Otherwise, a maximum of effort will produce no results, but more commonly wrong and undesired results.

*Management* by *objectives* is an administrative process rather than a political process. This makes it all the more important to focus on understanding as the first management result—bringing out the basic views, the basic dissents, the different approaches to the same task and the same problem within the organization.

The major departments of the federal government that have been created in the last twenty years: the Department of Defense, the Department of Health, Education, and Welfare (HEW), the Department of Transportation, and the Department of Housing and Urban Development (HUD), are commonly criticized for being ineffectual as well as administrative labyrinths. They are often contrasted, to their detriment, with older agencies such as the Department of the Interior or the Department of Agriculture, which, it is alleged, are so much more effective. The reason usually given for the lack of effectiveness of these newer agencies is "lack of direction" or "internal division." What made these older agencies effective, especially in the New Deal days when they reached a peak of effectiveness, was, however, the intelligent use of informed dissent on the part of the men who led them. Harold Ickes in Interior or Henry Wallace in Agriculture took infinite care to produce informed dissent within the organization and thus to obtain understanding for themselves and to create understanding for their associates. Thus, when decisions on goals and priorities were made unilaterally by the top man himself, and by no means democratically, they were understood throughout the organization; the top man himself understood what alternatives were available, as well as the position of his people on them.

Similarly, the Japanese system of "decision by consensus" is often cited these days as an example for the American decision maker. However, the Japanese do not make decisions by consensus, rather they deliberate by consensus. The seemingly long gestation period of a decision in Japanese organizations is devoted to bringing about the maximum understanding within the organization and to enabling those who are going to have to participate in the subsequent action to express their own views of the issue and their own definitions of the question. Consequently, they find out where their colleagues and associates stand, what they feel, and how they feel. Then a decision can be reached which the organization understands, even though large groups within it do not necessarily agree or would have preferred a different decision. Perhaps the greatest strength of the Japanese process is that priorities can actually be set and be made effective.

The second management result of management by objectives is to produce *responsibility* and *commitment* within the organization; to make possible *self-control* on the part of the managerial and professional people.

The advocate of MBO likes to talk about "participation." This is a misleading term, or at least an inadequate term. The desired result is willingness of the individual within the organization to focus his or her own vision and efforts toward the attainment of the organization's goals. It is ability to have self-control; to know that the individual makes the right contribution and is able to appraise himself or herself rather than be appraised and controlled from the outside. The desired result is commitment, rather than participation.

For this reason the usual approach of MBO toward goal-setting for the individual or for the managerial component is inadequate and may even do damage. Usually MBO says to the individual manager, Here are the goals of this institution. What efforts do you have to make to further them? The right question is, What do you, given our mission, think the goals should be, the priorities should be, the strategies should be? What, by way of contribution to these goals, priorities, and strategies, should this institution hold you and your department accountable for over the next year or two? What goals, priorities, and strategies do you and your department aim for, separate and distinct from those of the institution? What will you have to contribute and what results will you have to produce to attain these goals? Where do you see major opportunities of contribution and performance for this institution and for your component? Where do you see major problems?

Needless to say, it is then the task of the responsible administrator to decide. It is not necessarily true, as so many romantics in management seem to believe, that the subordinate always knows better. However, it is also not necessarily true that the boss always knows better. What is true is that the two, subordinate and boss, cannot communicate unless they realize that they differ in their views of what is to be done and what could be done. It is also true that there is no *management* by objectives unless the subordinate takes responsibility for performance, results, and, in the last analysis, for the organization itself.

The next results are *personnel decisions*. As stated earlier, MBO requires allocation of resources and concentration of effort. *Management* by objectives should always result in changing the allocation of effort, the assignment of people and the jobs they are doing. It should always lead to a restructuring of the human resources toward the attainment of objectives. It is not true, though administrative routine believes it, if only subconsciously, that every existing job is the right job and has something to contribute. On the contrary, the ruling postulate should be: Every existing job is likely to be the wrong job and needs to be restructured, or at least redirected. Job titles may be sacred, and in every large organization there is an unspoken but fervent belief that the Good Lord created section chiefs. In reality, job substance changes with the needs of the organization; and assignments, that is, the specific commitment to results, change even more frequently.

Job descriptions may be semi-permanent. However, assignments should always be considered as short-lived. It is one of the basic purposes of managerial objectives to force the question, What are the specific assignments in this position which, given our goals, priorities, and strategies at this time, make the greatest contribution?

Unless this question is being brought to the surface, MBO has not been properly applied. It must determine what the right concentration of effort is and what the manpower priorities are, and then convert the answers into personnel action. Unless this is done, there may be objectives but there is no management.

Similarly important and closely related are results in terms of *organization structure*. If the work in organization over the last forty years has taught us anything, it is that structure follows strategy. There are only a small number of organization designs available to the administrator. How this limited number of organization designs is put together is largely determined by the strategies that an organization adopts, which in turn is determined by its goals.

*Management* by objectives should enable the administrator to think through organization structure. Organization structure, while not in itself policy, is a tool of policy. Any decision on policy, that is, any decision on objectives, priorities, and strategies, has consequences for organization structure.

The ultimate result of *management* by objectives is *decision*, both with respect to the goals and performance standards of the organization and to the structure and behavior of the organization. Unless MBO leads to decision, it has no results at all; it has been a waste of time and effort. The test of MBO is not knowledge, but effective action. This means, above all, risk-taking decisions.

The literature talks about MBO often as a "tool for problem solving." However, its proper application is as a means of problem definition and problem recognition. Perhaps even more important, it is a means of problem prevention.

Thus, MBO is not a procedure to implement decision, a systematic attempt to define, to think through, and to decide. Filling out forms, no matter how well designed, is not management by objectives and self-control. The results are!

MBO is often called a tool of planning. It is not the same thing as planning, but it is the core of planning. MBO is usually called a management tool. Again, it is not all of management, but it is the core of management. It is not the way to *implement* decisions on policy, on goals, on strategies, on organization structure, or on staffing. It is the *process* in which decisions are made, goals are identified, priorities and posteriorities are set, and organization structure designed for the specific purposes of the institution.

It is also the process of people integrating themselves into the organization and directing themselves toward the organization's goals and purposes. The introduction of MBO into public service institutions, especially into governmental agencies during the last few years, may thus be the first step toward making public service institutions effective. So far it is only a first step. What has been introduced so far, by and large, is the procedure, and there is danger in procedure being mistaken for substance. Yet the great need of the public institution is not procedure. Most of them have all the procedures they need—the great need is performance. Indeed, performance of the public service institution may be the fundamental, the central, need of modern society. Management by objectives and self-control should help fill a good part of this need. However, its success depends upon the administrator: in applying MBO, he or she must obtain the right results, both with respect to *objectives* and to *management*.

# CHAPTER SIX

# The Coming Rediscovery of Scientific Management

EVERYBODY "KNOWS" THE FOLLOWING "FACTS" about Frederick Winslow Taylor: His aim was "efficiency," which meant reducing costs and increasing profits. He believed that workers responded primarily to economic incentives. He invented the "speed-up" and the assembly line. He saw only the individual worker, and not the work group. He considered workers to be "machines" and to be used as machines. He wanted to put all power and control into the hands of management, while he had deep contempt for the workingman. And he was the father of "classical organization theory," with its hierarchical pyramids, its concept of the span of control, its functions, and so on.

But even the most cursory reading of Taylor* immediately shows that every one of these "well-known facts" is pure myth.

---

First published in *The Conference Board Record*, June 1976.

*Taylor's three works on "scientific management" are *Shop Management*, published in 1903 under the auspices of the American Society of Mechanical Engineers, after having been read at a meeting of the Society in June 1903, in Saratoga, New York; *Principles of Scientific Management*, written in 1909, for publication by the American Society of Mechanical Engineers, but withheld by the Society as not

Taylor's central theme, which he repeated again and again, was the need to substitute industrial harmony for industrial warfare and mutual trust for fear in the industrial plant. This required, he maintained, four major changes:

1. It first required high wages. Indeed, Taylor demanded of every management starting to introduce "scientific management"—that is, the systematic study of work and tasks—that it commit itself at the outset, before beginning the study itself, to a wage increase of 30 to 100 percent. And in his first attempt to describe what he then called the "task system" in *Shop Management*, he stated almost at the outset: "This book is written mainly with the object of advocating *high wages*—as the foundation of the best management."

   He believed that productivity brought about by doing work right would make possible high wages and would, in effect, provide what we today would call "affluence." And Taylor strongly believed that the worker should receive the *full* benefit of higher productivity obtained through "scientific management," whether in the form of higher wages or of shorter hours.

   Yet Taylor did not believe that economic incentives by themselves would motivate. He anticipated practically all the later research of the human relations school or of Frederick Herzberg in stating that higher wages by themselves do not provide motivation, but that dissatisfaction with wage incomes is a major deterrent and destroys motivation. (The word "motivation" was, of course, unknown to Taylor—it did not come into general usage until the twenties; Taylor speaks of "initiative.")

---

"scientific" enough, whereupon Taylor circulated it privately in 1911 and then authorized Harper & Brothers to publish it; and his most comprehensive statement, his five-day Testimony, from January 25 to January 30, 1912, before a Special Committee of the House of Representatives. All three documents have been collected in one volume, *Scientific Management*, published by Harper & Row first in 1947, and reprinted many times since. All quotations in this essay are taken from this volume.

2. The second major need, according to Taylor, was to eliminate physical strain and bodily damage caused by doing the work the wrong way. Again and again, he pointed out that "scientific management" lightened the heavy physical toil and maintained energy. Again and again, he pointed out how traditional work creates injuries, fatigue, strain, dulls the faculties, and wears out the body. In a passage in the introduction to *Principles of Scientific Management*, which sounds strangely contemporary, Taylor contrasts the then-popular concern with the wanton destruction of such physical resources as forests, coal, or oil with the disregard of the wastage and destruction of the human resource.

3. Thirdly, Taylor believed that "scientific management" would produce industrial harmony through providing the means for the fullest development of the human personality. In his Testimony he said:

> *It becomes the duty of those on the management side to deliberately study the character, the nature, and the performance of each workman, with a view to finding out his limitations, on the one hand, but even more important, his possibilities for development on the other hand; and then, as deliberately and as systematically as possible, to train and help and teach this workman, giving him, wherever it is possible, those opportunities for advancement which will finally enable him to do the highest and most interesting and most profitable class of work for which his natural abilities fit him and which are open to him in the particular company in which he is employed. This scientific selection of the workman and his development is not a single act; it goes on from year to year and is the subject of continual study on the part of the management.*

Taylor not only preached this, he practiced it. One of his most interesting innovations, and one on which he insisted in every plant in which he introduced "scientific management," was the appointment of people whose main duty it was to identify abilities in the work group and to help workers acquire the training and the skill for advancement to better, more highly skilled, more responsible, and, above all, bigger jobs. He insisted—most successfully in his work at Bethlehem Steel—that no one be fired as a result of "scientific management," but that attrition and normal turnover be used to place the workman in another job in the plant. Again and again, he stressed the need to enrich jobs and work and to make them bigger, rather than confine them to one repeated operation. And he stressed the duty of management to find what a man is suited for—and then to make sure that he gets to do this kind of work. Taylor maintained that except for those few capable of work but unwilling to do it, there are only "first-rate men." It is management's job to make sure that they get the opportunity to excel.

> 4. Finally, "scientific management" to Taylor meant the elimination of the "boss."

*If there is anything that is characteristic of scientific management, it is the fact that the men who were formerly called bosses under the old type of management, under scientific management become the servants of the workmen. It is their duty to wait on the workmen and help them in all kinds of ways.*

Moreover, what Taylor meant by "functional foremanship" is what we now call "matrix organization." He had nothing to do with "classical organization" and its "hierarchy"; it clearly runs contrary to Taylor's basic principles.

## The True Taylor

Contrary to everything one reads about Taylor, he was concerned neither with profits nor with costs. His concern was what we today would call "productivity" (a word unknown seventy years ago). Far from being an admirer of management, Taylor was exceedingly critical of it: "Nine-tenths of our trouble has been to bring those on the management side to do their fair share of the work, and only one-tenth of our trouble has come on the workmen's side."

He did not hesitate, in his Testimony, to speak of U.S. Steel's management as "deplorable" and indeed "shameful." He repeatedly, and with great bitterness, attacked the people in top management who refused to pay a worker more than the "going wage" and who opposed "scientific management" because a worker under it will immediately earn $6,50 a day, where the "going wage" at the time was $5 a day. He was forced out as superintendent of Midvale Steel—the company where he had begun as an apprentice journeyman at age eighteen and where he first developed what was later to be known as "scientific management"—because he insisted on giving the workers the full benefit of their increased productivity, rather than keep wages low and raise profits. Altogether, most managements of the time kept him out of their plants as a "dangerous radical" and "troublemaker."

Taylor strongly believed in teamwork. He went to great lengths, in his Testimony, to point to the Mayo Medical Clinic as the finest example of "scientific management" at work, because it had succeeded in enabling a group of ten physicians and surgeons to work together as one team.

Taylor equally did not, as everybody seems to believe, want to give management all the control and to divorce the worker from management. On the contrary, this is what he said—and practiced:

> . . . under this new type of management, there is hardly a single act or piece of work done by anyone in the shop which is not preceded and followed by some act on the part of one of the men in the management. . . . First the workman does something; then the man on the management side does something and then the workman does something; and under this intimate, close, personal cooperation between the two sides, it becomes practically impossible to have a serious problem.

Indeed, Taylor considered "scientific management" a joint task of management and workers.

Finally, Taylor had absolutely nothing to do with the assembly line. There is no shred of evidence that Otto Doering of Sears, Roebuck and Henry Ford, who—between 1903 and 1910—developed the first assembly lines in the mail order house and the automobile plant respectively, had ever heard of Taylor or of "scientific management." Taylor certainly had never heard of the assembly line. In 1911–12, when Taylor last wrote (he was only fifty-six years old by then, but already aging), the assembly line was still below the horizon. It did not become fully visible until after the end of World War I, by which time Taylor was dead. And there is ample reason to believe that Taylor would have been highly critical of the assembly line and would have considered it very poor engineering. It violates his basic principles: the freeing of the initiative of the individual worker; the strengthening of the work group; and, above all, the finding, training, and developing of the individual for the job he is best fitted for.

## Flying in the Face of Ignorance

There are few cases in intellectual history where what a man actually said and did, and what he is generally believed to have said and done, are so totally at variance. The question, therefore, is why Taylor is being so totally misrepresented.

The standard explanation is that he was a "captive of nineteenth-century psychology." But this is nonsense. The trouble with Taylor was that he was so far ahead of his time that no one— or very few people—listened, let alone understood what he was saying and doing. In many ways, indeed in most ways, Taylor was a strong believer in what is now called Theory Y. He stated again and again that management by fear was counter-productive. At times he sounds like McGregor, at others, like Argyris—in his constant criticism of the resistance of organization to accepting the worker as a human being, for instance. At times he sounds very much like Frederick Herzberg. He was concerned with the "quality of life." to use today's terminology. Early in his Testimony he said:

*Scientific management is not an efficiency device, not a device of any kind for securing efficiency. Nor is it any bunch or group of efficiency devices. It is not a new system of figuring costs; it is not a new scheme of paying men; it is not a piecework system; it is not a bonus system; it is not a premium system; it is no scheme for payment; it is not holding a stopwatch on a man and writing things down about him; it is not time study; it is not motion study nor an analysis of the movements of men; it is not divided foremanship or functional foremanship; it is not any of the devices which the average man calls to mind when scientific management is spoken of.* In essence, scientific management involves a complete mental revolution on the part of the working men—and on the part of those on the management side, the foreman, the superintendent, the owner of the business, the Board of Directors—as to their duties towards their fellow workers in the management, towards their workmen and toward all of their problems. *(emphasis added)*

But this was so far ahead of 1910 that few even heard what Taylor said. What people heard instead were the very things which Taylor asserted that scientific management is not. And to this day, those are the things which are taught in most engineering schools as "scientific management" and industrial engineering, and are stated in most books to be what Taylor stood for.

But Taylor also committed the unpardonable offense of proving the "isms" to be irrelevant—and for this neither the Right nor the Left will ever forgive him. The "system," Taylor implies, hardly matters. Job, task, and work do. The economy is not made by "capitalism" or "socialism." It is made by productivity. Taylor spoke of the "duty" of owners; he never spoke of their "rights." He spoke of the "responsibility" of workers; he never spoke of their being "exploited." In other words, Taylor did not hold the "system" responsible, nor did he expect any great change to come from, a "change in the system." His "revolution" was a "mental" revolution, and not a social one. This flew directly in the face of the most cherished beliefs of 1910—and it still flies in the face of the prevailing beliefs of today.

This would not matter so much if Taylor had not been successful. Wherever his approach has been applied, productivity has increased manyfold, workers' real wages have gone up sharply, hours have gone down, and the physical and mental strain on the workers has been reduced. At the same time, sales and profits have gone up and prices have gone down. The more successful Taylor is, the more hostile to him the prevailing ideologies must become.

Finally, there is the horrible fact that Taylor concerned himself with work. Taylor was the first man in history who actually studied work seriously. This is his historical importance. People had, of course, been talking about work since time immemorial. But no one had thought work worthy of serious study. Indeed, work was clearly beneath the attention of educated people.

Taylor was well aware of this: ". . . the professors of this country . . . resent the use of the word 'science' for anything quite so trivial as the ordinary, everyday affairs of life." But it was not just the use of the word "science," even in Taylor's definition as "classified or organized knowledge of any kind," which "the professors of this country" (we would say "the intellectuals") resent and reject. It is altogether the belief that work—sweaty, dirty, backbreaking labor such as shoveling sand or moving pig iron—offers intellectual challenge and could and should be pleasant, rewarding—both economically and psychologically.

"Professors" believe in "creativity." Taylor believed in systematic, hard, principled work. The "professors" believe in an "elite," no matter how much they preach "equality." Taylor did not believe in "equality." He knew that people differed in their abilities. But he considered everyone a "first-rate man" who did the job and task he was fitted for, and as such entitled to full opportunity, to a good income, and above all, to respect. Management had the duty, he thought, to find what each man was best fitted for, to help him to get there, and to enable him to perform and to achieve by organizing his task, by providing the tools and the information needed, and by giving him adequate managerial support and continuing training. But the "professors" of this world still tend to believe, albeit only unconsciously, that work is something slaves do.

## As the World Learns

Among the "makers of the modern world" Taylor is rarely mentioned. And yet he has had as much impact as Marx or Freud. To be sure, we have gone beyond Taylor and need to go beyond him. But to attack Taylor because he had, for instance, more faith in the power of reason to convince and to convert people than we, living after two world wars, can muster, is foolishness. It is very much like attacking Newton because he did not invent non-Euclidean geometry or discover the theory of relativity.

Taylor has triumphed, despite his detractors. He has triumphed where his main concern was—in manual work. When he predicted, in his Testimony, that "the workman of that day [a hundred years hence] will live as well, or almost, as a high-class businessman lives now, as far as the necessities of life and most of the luxuries of life are concerned," people laughed—yet this is, of course, exactly what has come to pass in the developed countries, and primarily as a result of the application of Taylor's principles. It has come to pass precisely the way Taylor predicted—namely, by "greatly increasing the output of the man without materially increasing his effort." It has come about because we have learned to study tasks, to organize them, to plan them, to provide the right tools and the right information—though no one would claim that we have reached perfection.

But Taylor's greatest impact may still be ahead. In the first place, the underdeveloped and developing countries are now reaching the stage where they need Taylor and "scientific management." They have now reached the stage where their main aim has to be higher wages and yet lower labor costs—that is, increased productivity of manual work. It is now as true of them as it was for the United States eighty years ago that "underproduction" is mainly responsible for the fact that, as Taylor said of America in 1900, "the poorer people have just so much fewer things to live on; that they have poorer food to eat; pay higher prices for their rent; can buy fewer clothes to wear than they ought to have; in other words, that they lack in many cases the necessities and in all cases the luxuries of life that they ought to have."

But the need to study Taylor anew and to apply him may be the greatest in the developed countries, that is, in the countries which have become developed because they have applied Taylor's principles to manual work. These are the countries in which Taylor now has to be applied to knowledge work.

## Making Mental Work More Productive

In his writings and in his Testimony, Taylor emphasized that no plant, no factory, and no railroad had used more than a few elements of "scientific management." The one perfect example of "scientific management" in action, which Taylor cited, was the Mayo Clinic (for which Taylor claimed no credit). Taylor himself, in other words, was fully aware that "scientific management" applies to knowledge work as well as to manual work.

To make knowledge work fully productive requires many things Taylor did not concern himself with. It requires objectives and goals. It requires priorities and measurements. It requires systematic abandonment of the tasks that no longer produce and of the services that are no longer needed. It also requires organization, largely along the lines of the "matrix organization" which Taylor reached for in his "functional foremanship."

But making knowledge work productive also requires "task study" and "task management." It requires the analysis of the work itself. It requires, understanding of the steps needed, their sequence and their integration into an organized process. It requires systematic provision of the information needed and of the tool needed. All of these are concepts of "scientific management." It does not require "creativity." It requires the hard, systematic, analytical, and synthesizing work which Taylor developed to deal with shoveling sand, lifting pig iron, running paper machines, or laying brick.

Knowledge work already has the high wages which were Taylor's aim. Now it has to achieve the productivity which alone can justify the high wages. And this requires, above all, changes in "mental attitudes" and Taylor's "complete mental revolution" on the part of both the knowledge worker and his management.

The need today is neither to bury Taylor nor to praise him. It is to learn from him. The need is to do for knowledge work and knowledge worker what Taylor, beginning a century ago, did for manual work and manual worker.

# CHAPTER SEVEN

# The Bored Board

HELP WANTED

Major multi-billion dollar corporation seeks professional member on board of directors. We have job enrichment plan to convert position from rubber-stamping to active policy-making. Requires 40–50 days per year intensive work. Salary high. Rare opportunity. Corporation presidents, attorneys need not apply.

The "help wanted" advertisement above is the kind of statement I would make to a prospective candidate for a board of directors. I would tell him I'm not just looking for new blood, but I'm going to redesign the whole body—because when boards were conceived several hundred years ago, nobody envisioned the world in which they misfunction today.

All over the Western world boards of directors are under attack and are being changed. In the countries of Germanic Law—Germany, Holland, Austria, and Scandinavia—there is "co-determination," that is, labor union representation on company boards. In Sweden, the

---

First published in *The Wharton Magazine*, Fall 1976.

government appoints public representatives to the boards of big companies. In the United States, increasing numbers of large companies put "representatives" of various "minority" groups—blacks, or women, or consumers—on their boards. Increasingly they elect "public members" to represent the "public interest."

These changes are by no means confined to the boards of businesses. There is perhaps even more pressure for changing the conventional boards of universities, of hospitals, and of professional societies. One of the first acts of Jerry Brown, when elected governor of California, was to put a student representative on the Board of Regents of the University of California. In the American Medical Association, one of the biggest fights in recent years centered on the demand of the young doctors in training, the interns and residents, for representation on the AMA board—a fight they eventually won. Now they are pressing for board membership in hospitals.

All these pressures assume that the board matters. They assume that the board of directors or of trustees, whether of a business, a university, or a service institution, is truly the "governing organ."

But there is little evidence to support this assumption. On the contrary, years of experience indicate that the board has become a *roi fainéant*, an impotent ceremonial and legal fiction. It certainly does not "conduct the affairs of the enterprise"—neither in this country nor in Europe. Life on the board is not juicy and exciting. Rather, it is dull. Board members are more often bored by routine than stimulated by manipulating the levers of power.

In every major business catastrophe of the last forty or fifty years, from the collapse of the Austrian Credit Anstalt in 1931, which forced Britain off the gold standard and triggered the collapse of the American banking system, down to such recent debacles as Penn Central or Franklin National Bank, the board members were apparently the last people to be told that anything was awry. Similarly, in the student uprising of the late 1960s, the university boards were taken completely unawares, without the slightest intimation that trouble was brewing. Hospital boards—which, according to law, own the hospital, have all the power, and make all the decisions—rarely get involved in the debates over the costs, the control, and the policy of hospitals.

And the boards were just as ignorant, uninformed, and impotent in the bribery scandals of business. That Lockheed was handing out bribes, thinly disguised as "commissions," was an open secret long before it hit the headlines in 1975–76. The only important people who did not know about it, apparently, were the Lockheed directors. The same ignorance and impotence were displayed by the boards of Northrop and Gulf Oil in the bribery scandals of those firms. Managements clearly saw no reason to inform their boards and boards saw no reason to ask—and would not have received an answer had they asked.

Some board members, aware of their powerlessness, are beginning to complain that they serve no function and are kept busy with trivia, even when they want to do serious work. I, for instance, served for six years on the board of a fast-growing state university in New Jersey. The board members were genuinely interested in the university. Most of them had considerable experience in teaching, research, and administration. Others had held significant political office. The board met at least once a month, around 5 p.m., and was usually still at work at midnight. Yet we rarely got to the subjects that were uppermost in the minds of the board members: educational policies; the direction of the college; or the relationships between administration, faculty, and students.

Instead, our time was taken up with maternity leaves for Spanish instructors, waiving of fees for foreign students, promotions of people we had never heard about, or the acquisition of real estate for a new parking lot. We often tried to get to the matters we knew to be important, matters in which we also considered ourselves to be competent. But each time we were sternly reminded by the representative of the State Board of Higher Education (who sat in on every meeting) that state law restricted us to the tedious trivia. She told us at the same time, however, that state law mandated maternity leaves, promotions, and parking lots, so they would go through no matter how we voted.

The same situation exists even in large businesses. Board meetings rarely go beyond similar trivia: approval of a raft of promotions which have already become accomplished fact; approval of short-term budgets which few of the board members can possibly understand, let alone analyze in depth; approval of last month's operating results, when they have become past history; or spirited debates over a branch manager's right to sign checks.

Many board members I meet have their own stories of frustration, of confusion, of wasted time. Quite a few, including myself, are no longer willing to serve on boards, because we do not think we can contribute anything in such circumstances.

If boards are to function with a serious purpose, some major changes are needed. Simply changing the membership of a board does not make the board more effective. For example, the managers of German industry vocally oppose extension of co-determination. But every German manager I talked to asserted that co-determination has made no difference whatever in the way his board works—or rather, does not work—and in the way he runs his company. Similarly, the array of board members representing minority groups or women—or even consumers—on American boards has not made any noticeable difference in the way the companies are being run.

The crisis of the boards is not, as the current discussion tacitly assumes, a problem of the "right people." Whenever an institution malfunctions as consistently as boards of directors have in nearly every major fiasco of the last forty or fifty years, it is futile to blame men. It is the institution that malfunctions. The large complex organization—whether business enterprise, university, or hospital—has changed so much that the traditional board, which law and custom envisage, no longer works and no longer can work.

The rules for boards in our corporation law—in this country as well as in western Europe—were written in the middle of the nineteenth century. They assume a business which is small and regional, if not local. It has one or two products. It is owned by a very small number of individuals, either the people who started it or their descendants. In turn, their stake in the business is the major, if not the only, property of these people or their families. So they have a strong interest in its performance and success. In such a situation the board can be what the law expects it to be, i.e., knowledgeable and close to the affairs of the business. And it can give direction to management.

But this is a very different institution from the multinational corporation, with a multiplicity of markets, products, and technologies; with plants in twenty countries, research laboratories in five countries, and sales forces in sixty countries; with a complex management structure, and with its controlling ownership (as in all publicly held big American businesses) in the hands of one hundred or more employee pension funds, that is, in the hands of "trustees" rather than of "owners."

The university board dates back to the small denominational college and was originally meant to link a Protestant congregation to its own educational institution. Contrast this with today's "multiversity," with its 25,000 students, 4,000 teachers, and 8,000 other employees; its 6 layers of vice presidents, deans, and chairmen; its 40 schools and major departments; and its $100 million budget. Yesterday's board becomes a stale joke.

The hospital board still reflects the time—less than a century ago—when the hospital was primarily a place for the poor to die in a little decency. In those days a hospital board charged with soliciting charitable donations from the community made sense. Today's hospital is the community's center of health care and advanced medical technology. It is also the most complex human institution around, with a profusion of services and health care professions which nobody dreamed of even fifty years ago. Nearly all of its revenue comes from "third party payments"—from the government, from Blue Cross, or from private health insurance—rather than from charity or direct patient fees. A board composed of well-meaning local citizens willing to lend their names to fund-raising efforts is hardly appropriate.

Surely, the board cannot do what the law says it should do, that is, to "manage." Managing any of today's complex institutions is a full-time job and not for amateurs, even if well-meaning, responsive, and experienced in running their own institutions.

But where does that leave the board? Does it have any function at all, or is it obsolete?

Two such totally different people as John D. Rockefeller, Sr., the father of the Standard Oil Trust of American folklore and history, and Franklin D. Roosevelt, father of the New Deal, considered traditional boards to be pure excess weight. Both tried to eliminate them. Rockefeller had to have a board for his company—the law demanded it. But he got around the law by creating the "inside board" of company executives, who met about once a week but were managers the rest of the time. Franklin D. Roosevelt, when setting up the Tennessee Valley Authority (TVA), vetoed an outside part-time board of directors. Instead he gave the TVA the Rockefeller-style kind of "inside board" of full-time managers. Both men used the same argument: "There is a management job to be done. It requires full-time work and exclusive concentration on the affairs of the enterprise. Part-time outsiders need not apply."

The only function the current board has, many executives argue, is the function which the American Constitution assigns to the Vice President: to stand by without a real job until there is a succession crisis. Modern boards tend to swing into action only when management collapses, either through death of the incumbent or because of his total failure.

Despite the anachronistic appendage which most boards have become, there is need for a truly effective, truly independent outside board for the large complex institution, whether private business or public service. The need is not primarily rooted in the "public interest" or in the wish to make boards "democratic." The need is, above all, a need of the institution itself: it cannot function well in all its complexity unless it has an effective board.

If any proof of this were needed, the bribery scandals of recent years, e.g., Lockheed, would supply it. Here was not a management looting a company; on the contrary, what the management did was intended to advance the interests of the company and of its employees—and, in respect to sales of military aircraft, even the interest of the country, of its foreign policy and of its balance of payments. No law could possibly have prevented such actions. Yet any objective outsider would have seen, almost at once, that these bribes were both grossly unethical and grossly irresponsible—and would, in the not-so-long run, inevitably damage the company if not wreck it. This kind of irresponsibility—and well-meaning irresponsibility is the worst kind—only an outside board can prevent.

There are six essential functions only an effective board can discharge.

First, institutions need strong, competent management. Only a strong, effective, and independent board can ensure management competence. A strong board is needed to remove a top management that is less than fully competent. And only a strong board can force incumbents to make adequate plans to prepare, train, and test successors to top management.

Our society depends far too much on our big and complex institutions to leave top management to chance. Yet today, especially in the large publicly owned company, the chief executive officer, once installed, can be removed only through disaster or coronary thrombosis. It is the rare board that dares to remove a president who is merely incompetent, let alone one who is merely mediocre. Yet all the various constituencies of our important institutions (whether shareholders, employees, customers, or taxpayers) must be reasonably certain that management is truly accountable to an effective independent organ of supervision, audit, and control—that is, to a genuine board.

Second, an independent organ is needed to make sure that crucial questions are being asked: What is our business and what should it be? What is our mission? What are valid "results" in this undertaking? Who are our publics and our constituencies, and what can they legitimately expect from this institution? What are the major directions for the future? What should be abandoned or deemphasized? What new things are needed?

Then there are questions about the basic survival needs of the institution. How much innovation does it need so as not to become obsolete? What is the minimum growth needed not to become marginal in the market? How does one distinguish between growth that adds strength and performance capacity and growth that is merely fat (as was so much of the growth of the 1960s in all institutions)? Or growth that is, in effect, degenerative malignancy? How much profit is needed to earn the cost of capital, provide the premium for the risks of the future, and the capital needed for the jobs of tomorrow?

To be sure, only management can *answer* these questions. But somebody has to make sure they are being asked and thought about. Managements tend to postpone them for a perfectly good reason. After all, they first have to operate the day-to-day affairs of the institution. And the one predictable thing in any institution—especially in large and complex ones—is the daily operating crisis.

Third, an institution needs a "conscience." It needs a keeper of human and moral values and a court of appeal against tyranny and caprice or the equally harmful indifference of bureaucratic routine. It needs someone outside the daily work and the daily relationships who is concerned with what the institution stands for, what its values are, what it considers "right" and "wrong." In the large and complex institution, the chief executive officer is rarely able to play this role, if only because he may have to support: his management associates even when he thinks them sloppy, wrong, or callous. He has to live with them, after all. The conscience function needs someone who can act independently and can afford to rule against even the most powerful and most valuable people in the organization. Yet in the Lockheed and in the other bribery scandals, "conscience" questions were clearly never asked by the various boards—just as they are almost never asked by hospital or university boards.

This requires that board members regularly meet with people other than the organization's top management: with middle managers, foremen, and union stewards; with faculty and students; with interns, residents, nurses, and physical rehabilitation people. Their main job in these relationships is to listen, if only to learn what is being done right and where the strengths lie. Primarily, it is the board's job to make clear, often by its presence alone, that someone is concerned with values, with standards, and with justice.

Almost all executives will recoil at this idea. They will claim that a board "doing an end run around management" undermines management's authority. The danger does exist. Yet America's oldest board, the Overseers of Harvard, has done just that for three hundred fifty years without disrupting the university. Most of the thirty Overseers—each an alumnus and elected by the alumni—spend around fifteen days a year as members of a "Visiting Committee" of a school or department. They sit down with the faculty and, very often, with students, auditing the level and direction of instruction and research, listening to ideas, proposals, and complaints, and then reporting back to the full Board of Overseers and the university's administration. Apart from money raising, this is the principal activity of the Overseers.

Fourth, management itself needs an effective outside board. Top-level managers need people with whom they can talk in confidence, can deliberate, can think aloud. They need people with whom they can share their questions, doubts, and uncertainties. Within a large organization, no matter how "permissive" or how "democratic," the top people are, of necessity, both isolated and rigidly circumscribed. Any chief executive must be on his guard when discussing his thoughts with his associates or subordinates.

For every large organization is a rumor mill, which interprets or misinterprets even the most casual comment by the top man and treats it as a command or a decision.

Yet the most "decisive" chief executive cannot reach a decision without a lot of doubt and hesitation, without weighing alternatives, without arguing with himself. An effective board which understands the institution, its opportunities, and its problems—and yet is detached from the problems themselves—will not relieve the chief executive of the "loneliness of command." But without a genuine council, top management people become prisoners of their own positions.

Fifth, the management of a large institution needs windows that open on the outside world. Inevitably, it sees its own institution as large and important, and the rest of the world as small—if it sees the rest of the world at all. Yet the "hospital mind," the "college mind," and the "business mind," while inevitable, are just as limited as the "military mind" of the generals. The top people in a large and complex organization cannot easily get to the "real world" outside. Therefore, they need to make sure that the real world can get to them. They need channels of outside perception. (The great masters in building them, by the way, were two American presidents—Abraham Lincoln and Franklin D. Roosevelt—who consulted their "kitchen cabinets" of independent outsiders to the constant chagrin and scandal of their official cabinet colleagues.)

Finally, the large institution needs to be understood by its constituencies and by the community. No outsider really understands what goes on "on the fourteenth floor" or "in the president's office." What is so obvious to the decision maker in the executive suite is usually not perceived by the public outside, beginning with people in responsible positions within the organization.

These functions require a very different board than the one we inherited from the nineteenth century. Above all, boards need to accept the idea that they have a responsibility and, with it, specific work of their own. Otherwise, they will not accomplish anything.

The first priority in modernization is not to change the board's membership. The first priority is to change the board's role, function, and work.

Perhaps the most important thing is to relieve boards of most—in some cases, of all—chores they are loaded down with today. Most of them are trivia. If the board should discuss them at all, three hours once a year should suffice.

Then comes the job of developing the proper work plan for the board—the systematic review of executives and their performance; the systematic review of plans, policies, and direction; the systematic thinking through of major decisions. It is not enough even for the ablest board to sit down once a month with an agenda prepared by top management and simply give of their wisdom and counsel. The board has to work. There must be objectives and goals against which the board can measure its own performance—something practically unheard of today. In the larger and more complex institutions the board probably needs a small staff of its own just as, for instance, congressional committees have developed staffs of their own.

Who belongs on a board? Let's start with some negatives. Most of the people who traditionally sit there do not belong on boards at all. No one who is a supplier, whether of goods or of services, should sit on the board of an institution from which he expects to get paid. This rules out the lawyer, the banker, the broker, and the consultant. They are all in potential conflict of interest between their role as a supplier and their board membership. The guiding rule should be that of the public accountant whose canon of ethics forbids him to serve on the board of any company he or his firm might audit.

Retired officers of a company do not belong on the board. If their experience and counsel is to be put to productive use—and this is often highly desirable—we might adopt the Japanese practice and retain them as "counsellors." But one cannot "retire" and still oversee one's successor.

Even the most highly sought-after board member—the president of a company of equal size but in another field—has no business being on any board. Running a company, even a medium-sized one, is far too demanding to leave time for the systematic work which board membership requires. There is altogether too much to be done to want a board member, no matter how able, who sits on a great many of them—a Hermann Abs, for instance, the former head of Germany's largest bank, who sat on about one hundred and fifty company boards at the same time.

It is much less clear who does belong on a board. One reason is that the same board needs two different kinds of people.

The first kind are representatives of the constituencies—investors, employees, customers, and other groups in the community. Such people are needed not because institutions ought to "represent society." The institution needs them to bring the "outside world" into an isolated management's field of vision and perception, and also to provide communication to an increasingly fragmented public.

Both the European co-determination policies and the far more pragmatic American attempts to bring interest groups into board membership address a genuine problem. Of the two, perhaps the American approach, for all its bumbling improvisation, makes more sense. It recognizes that the modern institution has a great many different constituencies. Co-determination, on the other hand, subjects all groups and interests in the community and economy to the "producer interest" of investors and employees. I believe it is far more a "producer cartel" directed against the consumer than the "industrial democracy" it purports to be.

Interestingly enough, in most discussion about constituency representation, the biggest, most important, and least represented one is almost never mentioned. I mean the new owners of America's big businesses, the pension funds of the country's wage earners. Popular rhetoric accuses today's corporation boards of representing only the shareholders and ignoring society's other interests. Yet in the typical American corporation the major shareholder is not represented at all.

The pension funds today own around 30 percent of the equity of the listed corporations, and probably even more of the equity capital of the one thousand biggest ones. This is already enough to give them effective control. Within a few years, if only as a result of the recent Pension Reform Act, they are bound to own 50 percent or more. But the fund, while legally an owner, is actually an investor. The people who run it are trustees. They neither want to, nor are they entitled to sit on a board; to do so would be in violation of their fiduciary responsibility. Their duty is to sell a stock as fast as they can if they do not like a company, its prospects, or the way it is being managed.

But who then represents the owners, that is, the nation's employees and their pension funds? And how? This is one of the most important and most difficult problems we face in respect to the composition of our big-business boards.

No matter which constituencies we consider entitled to board representation, the members representing them will essentially be advisors rather than decision makers. For they stand in an inherent conflict of interests and loyalties between their duty as board members (that is, their duty to the institution) and their accountability to their constituents.

Let me illustrate. The chief executive of the seriously ailing Volkswagen company in Germany was forced out several years ago by the union members of his board because he proposed building an assembly plant in the United States. The American market, the union members agreed, was the only good market left for the "Beetle," which, while obsolescent and almost unsalable in Europe, was at that time still Volkswagen's mainstay. And German costs, the union members also agreed, had risen so much that Volkswagen's exports could not compete in the United States, or only at prices well below costs. Yet, the union members said, they could not vote for the best interest of the company even if its long-range survival were at stake. Instead, they had to vote according to the immediate interests of the Volkswagen workers, and therefore had to oppose the "exporting of jobs." Ten years later, even the union members of the Volkswagen board had to accept the need for a plant in the United States. But by then Volkswagen had also lost a good part of its American market. Whether it can regain it by building an American assembly plant ten years too late remains to be seen; for the market the union's shortsightedness lost for Volkswagen the Japanese now supply.

In this country, some of the blacks who have been elected to company boards see their role as representing the black community inside and outside the company. Others have said that being black has nothing to do with serving as a director; they consider the company's interest as paramount. But I personally know a number of highly competent black men and women who flatly refuse to serve on boards. They see no way of resolving the conflict.

The constituency representatives who come closest to understanding the problem are the trade union members on Swedish boards—ideologically, by the way, the furthest to the Left of any of the new breed among board members. When the law was passed which put their representatives on Swedish company boards, the trade unions organized a "school for company directors" with a faculty composed of Sweden's leading bankers, company presidents, and company directors. "Our members," one of their leaders explained to me, "have to learn how to serve the company on whose board they sit as expert advisors rather than continue to be spokesmen for labor; otherwise they'll lose all integrity and effectiveness right away."

A second kind of board member is also needed by the institution, its management, and society: the member who makes sure that there is effective top management; who makes sure that management thinks and plans; who serves as the "conscience" of the institution; as the counsel, the advisor, and informed critic of top management. Perhaps this might be called the "executive board." It is not a "managing" organ but is, in effect, the true "directing" organ.

In the larger and more complex institutions, these members will have to devote a great deal of time and work to their boards. Four to five days a month—forty to fifty days a year—might be the minimum. In other words, the task requires several "professional" members on every board. Each professional can serve only a very few institutions. They should be elected for a period long enough to become familiar with the institution, such as five or six years. They should probably not be eligible for immediate reelection so as not to become beholden to management. They should be well paid. A professional board member should earn from his four or five board memberships as much as a senior executive in a top management position.

Such professional board members are still quite rare. But the days of the amateur are clearly numbered. Both the Securities Exchange Commission and the courts are tightening up on the legal responsibilities of directors, to the point where it is getting far too risky to sit on a board except as a serious, time-consuming work assignment.

Board membership used to be a kind of private honor—unpaid, as a rule, but a badge of distinction. Boards used to be cozy places where one met once a month for a few hours and seconded the proposals of management. Changing such boards is not primarily a job to be done by law or by changing their memberships. It is a bigger job: to change the task and work of the board for the sake of the institution itself. It is primarily a challenge for top management. For management's own functioning and legitimacy will increasingly depend on an effective and independent board.

# CHAPTER EIGHT

# After Fixed-Age Retirement
# Is Gone

NO FORECAST I EVER MADE was greeted with greater derision than the prediction in the spring of 1976* that in another ten years, that is, by the mid-eighties, mandatory retirement age in America would be pushed beyond age sixty-five and that mandatory retirement at any fixed age might altogether be abolished.

Then it was believed almost universally that retirement would soon become mandatory at an earlier age than sixty-five, for the labor unions then were pushing hard for forced early retirement—at age sixty or, at the latest, age sixty-two.

Yet, within fifteen months after my book appeared, mandatory retirement was banned in our largest state, California. At the same time, the Congress of the United States was moving to raise the age to seventy. By now it is practically certain that mandatory

---

First published in *The Future of Business*, edited for Georgetown University by Max Ways (New York: Pergamon Press, 1978).

*In my book, *The Unseen Revolution: How Pension Fund Socialism Came to America* (New York: Harper & Row, and London: William Heinemann, 1976).

retirement at any one fixed age is on its way out and will disappear throughout the United States. This remarkable change, a shift by 180 degrees in national policies, was accomplished despite strong opposition from all "interests": labor, business, the government, and academia.

Although the policy reversal came suddenly, its causes—demographic, economic, and political—had been building up for many years. The new policy direction could have been predicted twenty years ago from trends that were reported in widely known statistics. Because the policy implications of these trends were not analyzed by government, business, unions, media, or academia, the United States is now ill-prepared to make major adjustments that the new policies will require. The nation has continued to view issues of retirement policy—and the more conspicuous issues of unemployment—with a mind-set shaped by the Depression. So rigid is the mental and emotional attitude that the leaders of American public opinion could ignore the vast changes that had occurred since the forties. Never was there a better example of the need for examining trends with a view toward foreseeing and tackling tomorrow's problems.

The present shift in retirement policy is only one—and not necessarily the most important—of a whole cluster of changes that will have to be made over the next decade in the way society looks at and deals with the central question of jobs. We are going to have to learn that "unemployment," the word that has dominated policy discussion for forty years, is no longer the central issue. The economy needs and can absorb more workers than it now has—provided the public and private framework of policy is altered to meet the actual conditions of the U.S. labor market. A brief review of what has happened to the fixed mandatory retirement age will give us a glimpse of the broader change—and the problems—that lie ahead.

Politically, the demand for a less rigid retirement age had become irresistible because of the growing power of older Americans.

People over sixty-five are the nation's fastest-growing "minority"—and indeed the only fast growing "minority." They are now more than one tenth of the population and will be one seventh in another ten years. They are a much larger proportion, however, of the working-age population. Increasingly, older people will become a major and highly powerful pressure group, that, unlike any other, cuts across all traditional political lines—whether economic, social, regional, sexual, or racial.

The change from fixed-age retirement to flexible-age retirement is inevitable. It is also desirable on human grounds. Mandatory retirement at age sixty-five condemns to idleness and uselessness a great many healthy people who want to work, if only part time. Sixty-five was established as America's mandatory retirement age more than sixty years ago, when both life expectancies and health expectancies were much lower. What was then, in 1920, age sixty-five now corresponds to age seventy-five or seventy-eight for men and age eighty for women. Conversely, the sixty-five-year-old today enjoys the health and life expectancy of the fifty-two-or fifty-three-year-old way back in the 1920s.

To be sure, a good many people in their sixties want to retire, but a large proportion of the people who retire—whether they take early retirement or keep on working until they are sixty-five—soon find that all they wanted was a long vacation. However, under the traditional policy of American Social Security and American pension plans, they cannot return to work without substantial penalties, if at all. To give people the option to postpone retirement, either by delaying mandatory retirement or by abolishing it altogether, was thus a belated adjustment to the great success of this century in extending life and health spans.

Economically also, later retirement and flexible retirement are highly desirable. Of the people in the United States now reaching retirement age, the great majority—three out of four or more—finished their education with junior high school or, at most, after a year or two of senior high school. They are people who worked mostly as blue collar workers in manufacturing, mining, or the services. Of the young people who now enter the labor force, about half have gone to school beyond high school and have at least some college. Very few of the new entrants into the labor force are, therefore, available for the jobs the retirees vacate. Altogether, we face a severe shortage of new entrants into the labor force, a few years down the road when the babies of the "baby boom" will all be in the work force—most of them are there already—and when the new entrants into the work force will be drawn from the babies of the years of the "baby bust," that began in 1960 and that cut the number of babies born by 30 percent. To some extent, this is being offset by the larger participation of young women in the work force—now as high as that of young men. But this shift has already been accomplished. From now on, for the next twenty years, the number of new entrants into the labor force will decline steadily, and the number of new entrants available for the jobs the retirees vacate will decline drastically.

The most obvious practical consequence of this change is that we cannot maintain mandatory retirement at age sixty-five and finance retirement pensions—whether through Social Security or through private pensions. In 1935, when Social Security was first enacted, there were nine Americans at work for every American over sixty-five. By 1977, the ratio had shifted to four-to-one. By 1985, it will be three-to-one. In addition, there are the "survivors," mostly widows who were far too old when their spouses died to reenter the labor force themselves. The dependency ratio—that is, the ratio between people in the labor force and people who have to be supported in retirement—is already as low as three-to-one; there are 92 million Americans at work and 32 million on retirement pensions or supported as "survivors." By 1985, that ratio will be down to two-and-a-quarter-to-one or so, unless retirement is delayed. This dependency ratio does not take into account the fact that a very large and growing proportion of the new entrants into the labor force, especially older married women, do not work full time.

On full-time equivalency, the dependency ratio is already well below three-to-one, which means that every American employed has to transfer about one third of his income, through Social Security taxes, through pension fund contributions, and increasingly through general taxes to support older people who are retired and on pension.

This is politically and economically unbearable. It means that the pension burden, whether carried by government or by the employer, is becoming increasingly the first charge on the economy, ahead of capital formation, ahead of maintaining and building plants and equipment, and ahead of creating new jobs. It also means that inflation becomes both absolutely inevitable and absolutely unbearable.

## The New Problems

Although abolishing fixed-age retirement is both inevitable and desirable, it creates serious problems. It confronts employers, labor unions, and governmental policy makers with entirely new challenges, for which none of them is in the least prepared.

1. The first of these challenges, and in many ways the thorniest, is that of establishing criteria for retiring people who have become physically or mentally incapable of continuing their work. If, as the California law clearly spells out, retiring people for age is no longer permitted, then there have to be objective criteria other than age—that is, physical or mental impairment. Who sets these criteria? Who administers them? The California law talks of "competence" to do the work. What is that? How is it defined? Who defines it?

    We know from industries that have criteria for retirement other than age., e.g., for airline pilots or locomotive engineers, that the criteria have to be set in advance. We know that they are best set by mutual agreement between employer and employee representatives. Indeed, we know that nothing so quickly creates a militant union as an attempt by the employer to set these criteria unilaterally and arbitrarily. And we know the criteria have to be administered impartially—that is, by outside professionals with or without representation by employer and employee. Above all, we know that the same criteria must apply regardless of age. If older people are being retired while younger people are allowed to continue to work at the same level and with the same abilities or disabilities, there is a *prima facie* case of discrimination. And if there are no criteria for "competence" at all for younger people and no regular review of their performance against the standards, no claim of "incompetence" against an older person, short of total paralysis or coma, is likely to be upheld. Indeed some unions, e.g., some Teamster's locals, are already saying that even a paraplegic, if only sufficiently old, will have to be kept on the payroll—"there is always something he can do."

For jobs which require physical capacity capable of being defined—response time for airline pilots, for instance, or visual acuity—these standards are not much of a problem, though it will be years before they have been worked out. But what about jobs in which the requirements are judgment, ability to cooperate with people, ability and willingness to listen to new ideas, performance in the classroom, and so on? In other words, what about the jobs of knowledge workers, who increasingly are becoming the center of the American economy and the American labor force? No one has tackled standards for them as yet.

In universities, where a few distinguished faculty members are being kept on annual contract beyond the traditional retirement age, "subject to their physical and mental capacity to do the work," the decision is usually left to the administrative officer, with or without the advice of a faculty group. There is almost never a decision to terminate; instead it is "suggested" to the colleague who has become senile that perhaps he better stop working. This will no longer be good enough. We urgently need due process that enables organizations to remove people who are no longer equal to the job, regardless even of contracts or academic tenure.

The problem now facing us is in respect to federal judges. When the Founding Fathers declared that judges could not be removed except by impeachment, they did not expect judges to live long enough to become senile—and now they do. We know that the federal judiciary will need to develop some self-controls. There will have to be some body—presumably a committee of the Judiciary Conference of the United States under the chairmanship of the Chief Justice of the Supreme Court—which can remove a judge who has ceased to be competent. How does one do this, however, with very large numbers of people—engineers, accountants, researchers, sales managers, professors, and so on? Without such a provision, only lawyers will benefit from the extension of working life.

We probably should maintain mandatory retirement for people in top jobs, though not mandatory retirement from work and job altogether. It is, I maintain, most undesirable for top people—whether in business, in academia, or in government— to continue indefinitely. A vice president of marketing who is fifty years old can be removed, even though it may mean buying up his contract. It makes no sense to have him become irremovable on his sixty-fifth birthday.

One reason why top people should not be allowed to stay on is that the one disease of which the patient himself is completely unaware is senility. If we leave it to older persons to decide for themselves when to quit top jobs, we risk senility in high places. There are already too many examples around of chief executive officers resisting retirement and staying on far too long. Sewell

Avery at Montgomery Ward, thirty years ago, is the usual example, of course. At the same time, there is no reason why the older and functioning person need stop working. There is no reason why the V.P. Marketing, if in full possession of his mental faculties, should not continue to work as a senior individual contributor—in charge of market research or customer relations or product development, for instance. What is needed is to get such a person out of the line of command or authority. Otherwise, the same rules should apply that hold for associates who do not hold top-level positions. We need to develop similar approaches regarding people who work for government or for universities and schools. We need to be able to move people out of top positions because their staying on is too risky and because there is need to make opportunities available to younger people. And we need to be able to keep such men and women in useful and productive work if they are mentally and physically able to continue working and want to do so.

2. Equally important, perhaps more urgent, is the question of the rights and benefits of the people who stay on beyond the age at which they could retire at a decent retirement pension. Neither American business nor American government has seen the problem involved in cases of this sort. Under present laws and union contracts, such people retain full seniority rights, including seniority rights to promotion and wage and salary increases. They retain full seniority in layoffs, even though they have an ample pension available to them. If we maintain this, we will see the ludicrous and inequitable result of keeping in full employment senior citizens whose children are grown up, who have no dependent parents, and who have available to them a retirement pension equal to their salaries (if only because of the lower tax burden and because of Medicare available to them), while laying off young adults, fathers of families with dependent children and dependent parents. This is, however, what the labor unions will

have to insist on, unless the employers today—in the private and the public sector—work out a more equitable system.

Under present laws and union contracts, such older people who stay on in work after they have reached the age at which their full pension benefits are available to them still will have to be provided with the full range of benefits and will carry the full load of benefits. The man or woman who stays on the job after age sixty-five pays, for instance, the full Social Security tax, as does the employer. A full contribution to the pension fund is being made, even though the employee's pension by that time is fully paid up. Under most health care plans, the employee who continues past age sixty-five still has to pay full Blue Cross and Blue Shield dues— or the corresponding insurance premiums—even though Medicare provides for reimbursement of most of his medical expenses, and indeed for more generous reimbursement than many health insurance plans do. This is clearly inequitable. It is unnecessarily expensive and high cost without benefit. It is also silly. Yet it will become a routine burden on both employer and employee unless employers and unions go to work now on adjusting their plans to the new reality, that is, to flexible retirement age.

The Japanese inadvertently solved the problem a long time ago. The Japanese official retirement age is fifty-five. It was set at that age level seventy years ago, when Japanese life expectancies were around forty-three years. Today, Japan has the same life expectancy as the West, so that the fifty-five-year retirement age has become an anachronism. Indeed, what the Japanese really have is not a retirement policy, but a "non-retirement" policy. The great majority of Japanese employees continue to work beyond age fifty-five, and a great many of them in the same job with the same employer as before. However, they are no longer "permanent" employees, but "temporary" employees—which means that they can be laid off if business slackens. They have no more job security. They have no more seniority. They no longer can expect a promotion or have a right to it. And their incomes go down by

30 to 40 percent. At the same time, these employees in many companies have a preferential right to be rehired should they want to come back from retirement and if physically and mentally fit, but only as "temporary" employees. The logic of this, according to the Japanese, is that people over age fifty-five, as a rule, no longer have dependent children or dependent aged parents. Their expenses are lower. The government, as it does in most countries, pays their health care bill. Yet they represent a valuable resource and one that few employers can afford to give up lightly.

3. Altogether, the abolition of fixed-age retirement—or the post-ponement of fixed-age retirement—will increasingly force employers to create permanent full-time jobs permanently staffed with part-time people, A good many older people will not want full-time jobs, and the older they get, the more likely are they to want part-time work. This is also true in respect to the other major source of new employees in the American work force—the older married woman. Increasingly, employers will have to learn to hire and put to work part-time people.

   In many ways, these part-time people are the most desirable employees. They do not, as a rule, move around much. Once they have it, they stay on the job. Their absenteeism and sickness record is remarkably good. They much prefer, as a rule, to go to work where their friends are to being alone at home with no one to talk to but the appliances. However, their attitudes are differ-ent. They do not, for instance, respond to traditional "supervi-sion." They have, after all, been working long enough, whether at the old job or in running a household, to know what work is and to have self-discipline.

   The part-time employee needs different benefits. The older employee, for instance, needs supplementary health insurance that covers what Medicare does not cover. He needs no unem-ployment insurance; he has Social Security or a company pension. The older married woman who works part time does not need any health insurance of her own if she is covered under her husband's policy. In other words, benefits have to be far more flexible to make sense. Under the present system, part-time people either enjoy no benefits (although benefits for them are predictably going to be a major union demand), or they enjoy benefits that do not, in fact, provide any benefit to them. How to give the part-time employee, whether an older person past traditional retirement age or an older married woman, the most for the dollars spent on benefits, is a major challenge, and one that employers and unions have not yet tackled.

Close to two fifths of the American labor force of tomorrow are likely to be part-time workers: older people past traditional retirement age, married women, and young people still in school and college. We are totally unprepared—indeed, totally unaware of this. To almost everybody, "labor force" still means male adults working full time. They actually comprise not much more labor force" (with another quarter or so rking full time).

ers and unions who are still imprisoned in ago. Our employment and unemploy- obsolete in that they fail to reflect the to a labor force in which a very large group—perhaps the largest single group—will be part-time people, many of whom have available to them economic support other than the income from their own work, whether Social Security and retirement pension, a spouse's wage and salary, or parental support. We do not even know the size of the labor force—we have a "body count" but no way to translate the numbers into full-time jobs able to be filled. Similarly, we have a total figure for people potentially available for *some* work—our so-called "unemployment figure"; but there is no clue in the figure to how many jobs the "unemployed" could fill since we do not know how many of them could take full-time work and how many only the most minimal of part-time work. We cannot even guess today at the amount of additional production we are losing because of unemployment; all the widely publicized figures of the "loss" suffered for lack of full employment are based on the untenable assumption that everybody reported as "available for work" and therefore as "unemployed" is available for forty hours of work a week. And we cannot even guess today at the economic hardship unemployment causes; we simply have no information regarding the other sources of income available to people who might take part-time jobs if available, whether retirement pay, a spouse's salary, parental support, or welfare and unemployment benefits.

This refusal to accept that the part-time worker, and especially the older part-time worker, has become a major element in the American labor force already grossly distorts economic perception and policy. It explains, for instance, why labor unions and liberal economists speak of "record unemployment," even though the real "record" of the last few years is the number and proportion of American adults at work, full time and part time. It also explains, however, why despite huge liberal majorities in the Congress, major "reflationary" policies have not been enacted—with a very large (though unknown) percentage of the "unemployed" available for part-time work only, there is little political pressure for "anti-depression" policies.

Our refusal to face up to the steady increase in part-time employees thus already impairs policy making. It will become a source of major mistakes as older people keep on working in large numbers, as they are bound to do now that fixed-age retirement is rapidly disappearing. Employers and unions, in particular, cannot afford to persist in believing that "employee" necessarily means "full-time worker"—yet both, by and large, are convinced that it does arid must mean just that.

4. Today, workers are encouraged to stay on the job or retire. Tomorrow, we will increasingly have to make it possible for people to move in and out of the labor force. Women, for instance, usually take a full-time job until the first child arrives. Then they usually drop out of the work (except in case of divorce) until the youngest child is eight or nine years of age. Then they work again, though often only part-time. However, people past traditional retirement age particularly will be disposed to being in-and-out workers. They do have a pension available to them. At the same time, many of them—perhaps a near-majority—will want to work. Today, the employee who retires, e.g., by taking early retirement, finds it very difficult to come back into the work force. Employers, as a rule, do not want him; he costs too much in pension contributions. For under our present system employers may not, under their pension plans, differentiate between employees who are dependent on the company's pension plan and employees who already have a pension and need, at best, a supplementary pension right. Social Security discourages people from working at any age once they have become entitled to even reduced Social Security benefits. Again, here is an area that needs new thinking lest the economy be saddled by high benefit costs that do not benefit anyone.

Specifically, we will have to think through Social Security. Our present Social Security system was enacted during the Great Depression of 1935, with the express purpose of moving as many people as possible out of the labor force. Increasingly, in the next ten years, we need the opposite policy—one that encourages people to stay at work. At present, anyone earning less than the median American income—that is, less than $14,000 per family—has powerful incentives to stop working when he reaches the age at which he is eligible for the full Social Security payment, that is age sixty-five. Social Security income is tax-free. Medicare is virtually free—also, of course, not taxed—and the individual increasingly has available to him some employer-paid pension, a good part of which is also not subject to taxation. If the older low-income employee gets a gross amount of 50 to 60 percent of his current wage in the form of Social Security and pension—and Social Security usually gives him 50 percent to begin with—he is today being penalized if he works and actually loses income.

What we need is a policy that encourages people to stay on the job and to remain economically productive—which also means producing taxes for the government. Such a policy must not penalize retirement, if only because this is not acceptable politically. We are indeed already on the road to such a policy— and pretty far down the road at that. People entitled to Social Security benefits now get larger checks the longer they post- pone drawing their Social Security pension. However, we still place a heavy penalty on working between the ages of sixty-five and seventy-two. Anyone in these years who earns income beyond a small amount loses all or almost all of his Social Security benefits, even though he has fully paid for them. And then, of course, he or she pays income, tax on the earnings received. Indeed, unless such a person makes a very high income—more than $20,000 a year—his earnings from his work is actually taxed at a 100 percent rate. Predictably, this is not going to last. Indeed, I would expect it to be changed before the end of the eighties.

5. The most difficult, but also the most important, problems now that fixed-age retirement is gone, confront us in the public sector. Private sector pension plans have problems, because people live so much longer than we expected even twenty years ago, and because of inflation. However, public sector pension plans, especially those of state and local governments, are a mess and are, in fact, generally bankrupt. It is reasonably certain that public sector employees face sharp cuts in what the public

increasingly feels are exorbitant pensions. I would, for instance, expect laws restricting government employees after retirement to the income (adjusted for taxes) they received before retirement. At present, a substantial portion of retired public sector employees enjoy larger post-tax incomes than the salaries they received while at work. This will be considered increasingly inequitable, but also increasingly incompatible with the survival of our states and cities and their financial viability.

At the same time, we impose severe and unjust penalties on the public service employee. Private sector employees have their pensions vested after a maximum of ten years of service—which means that after that period they have an account in their name, with pension rights defined and assured upon their reaching pensionable age. Public sector employees, and especially employees of state and local governments, have no such vesting. As a rule, they have no pension rights whatever, unless they have served a particular employer—a city or a state—for twenty years. Then they are entitled to a very large pension upon early retirement. The very large early retirement pensions are, in great measure, a form of reverse income distribution. They take money from the poor and give it to the rich. Typically, the police captain in a big city—such as Los Angeles or Detroit—goes into early retirement after twenty years of service and takes a job as chief of police in one of the affluent suburbs at a fraction of the salary the suburb would have to pay, did he not have his substantial early retirement pension from his first employer. As the big cities and the large state governments become increasingly insolvent under the pressure of unfunded or inadequately funded pension promises, the early retirement pension will come under increasing attack—and it cannot be defended.

At the same time, we will have to learn to vest public service pensions the same way we now vest private sector pensions. And in the public sector we will face the same problems of thinking through criteria for retirement, of the rights and benefits of people who work beyond traditional retirement age, of the part-time job, the in-and-out older worker, and so on, that we face in the private sector.

## The Need for Second Careers

The most important and the most novel of the challenges posed by the abolition of fixed-age retirement is the need for second careers for the middle-aged knowledge worker. It is a need which employers will very largely have to satisfy.

Increasingly, the abolition of fixed-age retirement will force employers to develop standards of performance, competence, and promotability for all knowledge employees, regardless of age. Also increasingly, the pressure will be on employers to remove in early middle age, that is, by age forty-five, the employee-accountant, training director, sales manager, engineer, or associate professor— who is no more than merely competent. Otherwise the employer will find that he cannot get rid of this employee at all. If he tries to do so, he will be guilty of "discrimination by age"—and the employer will no longer be able to say, as he does today, "Oh, well, he'll retire in a few years anyhow." The only thing he will be able to do is to place this employee in early middle age in another job and in another career.

The employee will also have a powerful incentive to want a second career once it is no longer taken for granted that one retires automatically at age sixty-five or sixty. Then the prospect of staying in the same place and on the same job for another two or three decades becomes a nightmare to the many middle-aged people who find themselves in a dead-end or deadening job.

Until the Pension Reform Act of 1974, these people rarely moved unless they were fired. They lost too much in pension rights. Now that pensions are vested after ten years of service, there is far more mobility in this group. With fixed-age retirement gone, this group is bound to need and to demand even more mobility—above all, organized placement efforts to give them second careers. The accountant who, after twenty years, is very tired of the steel company, is ready for a job as business manager of the community hospital. The assistant counsel in a company or in city government who won't make general counsel is ready for a partnership in a medium-sized law firm. The associate professor who has been teaching Introductory Japanese for twenty years and will never produce a scholarly book is ready to handle the liaison between a Japanese company and its Western joint-venture partners; and so on.

Systematic placement in second careers is commonplace in consulting and professional firms—management consultants, consulting engineers, law firms, and CPA firms. One of the country's leading executive recruiters, who specializes in finding technical and scientific personnel, has long insisted on being entrusted with the systematic "out placement" into second careers for the technical and scientific personnel of the companies for which he recruits. We know through these experiences that it takes only a few years for potential employers to realize that persons looking for a second career are not "misfits" or "failures." We also know that it takes organized efforts on the part of the employer to place the middle-aged employee in a second career. Indeed, we know that the smart thing to do is to find a number of potential employment opportunities for such people *before* telling them that they are going to be let go.

Far more important is that the abolition of fixed-age retirement will make a second career routine and commonplace. A goodly number of people will have multiple "career paths" from which to choose. For an increasing number of people will change careers, in their mid-forties and again when they reach their late sixties or early seventies and shift to part-time work.

In conclusion: flexible retirement is going to be the central social issue in the United States during the next decade. It is going to play the role that minority employment played in the sixties and women's rights played in the seventies. Yet employers, labor unions, and government policy makers pay no more attention to flexible retirement than they paid to minority rights in the forties and to women's rights in the fifties. This is going to be an expensive and dangerous neglect. The demands that the abandonment of fixed-age retirement will make—also the opportunities it will create—belong high on the priority list. They are demands arising out of great success.

For the extension of life span is the greatest achievement of this century. The demands that this success poses are comparatively easy to satisfy. The time to tackle them, however, is now—ten years from now they will have become "problems."

# CHAPTER NINE

# Science and Industry

## *Challenges of Antagonistic Interdependence*

SCIENCE AND INDUSTRY in the United States used to enjoy a relationship of mutual respect based on an unspoken conviction that they depended on one another. That relationship, while distant, was uniquely productive for both science and industry.

The first change in the traditional American relationship occurred after World War II. Research became fashionable in industry and government alike. These were the years when the stock market valued a company according to the amount of money it spent on research, and in which a lavish campuslike research center was considered proof of a management's competence. Similarly in those years—culminating in the space program of the 1960s—science and research increasingly came to be seen as the mark of the effective, well-planned, and properly progressive government program.

During the years after the war, the ability of America to convert science into industrial application was considered the outstanding

---

First published in *Science*, May 25, 1979.

strength of both American science and American industry. Treatise after treatise pointed out that the British, for instance, were America's equals in science. But the British failed to convert their own scientific achievements—in electronics, in polymer chemistry, in the computer, in radar, or in aviation—into technology, products, and economic advancement, whereas America did.

Equally, especially during the Truman and the Kennedy years, the willingness, indeed eagerness, of the American politician and government executive to apply science—"hard" as well as "soft"—to both the study of social and political problems and the design of social and political programs was seen both inside this country and outside as a distinct and great American achievement. The innovating ability of American society was widely explained throughout the world, including the Communist countries, as the result of the sensitivity of the American scientist to political and social needs and opportunities, and to the values and dynamics of the political process.

In quantitative terms, the relationship seems to be as close as ever—and perhaps even closer in computer sciences, solid-state and nuclear physics, the earth sciences, and biochemistry. It might be argued that nothing has really changed despite all the talk of the irrelevance of science or of the wickedness of "American imperialism" by the vocal critics on the New Left, despite Vietnam, despite inflation, and so on. One might indeed assert that the highly publicized and highly visible developments and media events—the headline- and demonstration-makers—are little more than whitecaps on the surface of the ocean.

Yet there has been a major change, not in the measurable realities of the relationship between science and the decision makers in industry and government, but in the moods, the values, and the meaning of the relationship. There is today distrust, disenchantment, mutual dislike even, and worse, lack of interest in each other on both sides. American scientists today, in large number, tend to suspect the traditional relationship as being tainted or impure.

Industry still professes to honor the relationship and to respect research. But industry's actions no longer fully live up to industry's professions. As to government, there is now a strong tendency to judge science by what is politically expedient or politically fashionable; that is, to attempt to subordinate science, whether pure or applied, to value judgments that are the reverse of, and largely incompatible with, any criteria one could possibly call scientific.

In both industry and government, there is even increasing doubt whether science and research do indeed lead to results. It is often argued that this reflects lengthening lead times, resulting from the increasing complexity and specialization of today's advanced scientific research. But there is no evidence that the lead times have lengthened; the time span between new theoretical knowledge and the first application is the same thirty to forty years that it has been all along (for example, between Maxwell's theory and Westinghouse, between X-ray diffraction and Carruthers' development of nylon and polymerization, or between quantum mechanics and semi-conductors). What is changing are not facts but faith. On both sides the mood is becoming one of alienation and perhaps even of recrimination. It is a dangerous mood, above all for American science and American scientists. Both sides stand to lose, but science stands to lose far more.

## Ways of Industry

The mind-set and values of industry—but equally of the government decision maker concerned with effective policy—are in danger of becoming hostile to the needs, the values, the goals, and the perception of science. One reason for this is the increasing pressure, especially in an inflationary period, to produce results fast. An inflationary period, by definition, is one that erodes and destroys both industrial and political capital. In an inflationary period, the existing value of future results is subject to the exceedingly high discount rate of inflation which, in effect, means that no results more than a year or two ahead have any present value whatever, whether value is defined in economic or in political terms. It is, therefore, not a period in which either industry or the policy maker can take risks.

Thus both industry and the governmental policy maker in an inflationary period concentrate on small, but sure and immediate, payoffs; that is, on what can be calculated with high probability. The application of true scientific knowledge is by definition a big gamble, in which payoffs are far in the future and thus exceedingly uncertain although very great in the event of success. In an inflationary period, the industrialist or the policy maker is almost forced into the small but quick payoff of a lot of small and, by themselves, unimportant projects that require very little science altogether and can only be damaged if exposed to too much science.

## Tax Effects and Investments

More important perhaps—or at least more insidiously deleterious over a longer period of time—is taxation. The tax system adopted by the United States in the last twenty years or so penalizes basic research and the adaptation of basic research to technology. Worse, through the combined working of corporation income tax and capital gains tax, the system greatly favors short-term, immediate gains and makes long-term investments in an uncertain future unattractive and unrewarding.

Equally inimical to investment in research and innovation is the increasing burden of regulation. It is not primarily that regulation adds cost, but that it creates uncertainty. Whether in respect to the environment, to safety, or to new drugs, regulation makes investment in research irrational, not only increasing the odds against research producing usable results but also making research into a crooked game.

Tax laws and regulations also push industry away from technology focus and toward financial conglomeration. Under the tax laws of the United States—laws which in this form do not exist in many countries—the proceeds of liquidating an obsolete business, product line, or technology are considered profit and are taxed as such both to the company and to the investor. Hence, businesses, instead of liquidating the obsolete, have to find new investments in new businesses for whatever cash is being released by the shrinkage of an old technology, an old product line, or an old market. And this, in effect, imposes conglomeration on them. This policy makes it increasingly difficult to shift resources from low and diminishing areas of productivity to areas of high and increasing productivity, and this impedes innovation. It also shifts businesses from a technological to a financial focus. It makes management increasingly a matter of finding the right financial investment.

## The Antitrust Bias

This constant pressure of the tax laws, which results in a swerve from the scientific and technological toward the financial and from the long term toward the short term, is then aggravated by the antitrust laws, which probably are responsible more than any single factor for turning American industry away from building on a technological, science-oriented base and toward the financially based conglomerate.

In the world economy, even businesses that are very large on the national scene are becoming marginal, if not too small. The "big business" of 1938 or even 1958 is a small, if not a marginal, business in the 1979 world economy. Yet our antitrust laws frown on the scaling-up of businesses except through the formation of conglomerates, which, however, lack the fundamental core of technological unity. This conglomerate is focused on financial rather than on technological results. Hence, investment in long-range research and in the application of scientific knowledge to economic production becomes difficult in the conglomerate. People who are good at building and running conglomerates are financially oriented people. Yesterday's business, with its unified technology, organized around a process, such as making glass, was basically technologically oriented and therefore looked to science for its future. The conglomerate, which comprises everything from tin cans and electronics to fast-food restaurants and dress shops, from airlines to banks and toys, is, of necessity, financially oriented. Research becomes a cost center rather than a producer of tomorrow's wealth.

Similar forces operate in government in respect to the interest and the investment in science. Even the most shortsighted businessman still has to focus on both the short term and long term. But a governmental budget is always myopic. It knows no time span other than the fiscal year. It has to justify allocation of resources on the basis of short-term and mostly political expediencies. This was one reason why some older and wiser heads in American science warned against dependence on government twenty-five years ago. Their fears proved well founded. As soon as science ceases to be an article of the faith and popular, and becomes *one* application of governmental funds rather than *the* application of governmental funds, the pressures of the budget process make science a low-priority choice for politician and bureaucrat alike.

There is also disenchantment with the results. Whether science oversold itself, or whether industry and government expected miracles, is beside the point; the results that business and government anticipated when they rushed into lavish expenditures on scientific research have rarely been attained. Surely, the relation between scientific work and results, whether in terms of goods, services, or such benefits as better schools or better health care, is far more difficult and complex than either scientist or policy maker thought.

As a result of these pressures and developments, industry and government are drifting toward what might be called a scholasticism of the budget, in which the budget is a closed system, with its own absolute logic.

Both the business executive and the governmental executive proclaim their faith in research, but neither can practice it today. The mind-set of executives, whether in business or in government, and their values thus inexorably shift from what Thorstein Veblen, about sixty years ago, called "the instinct of workmanship" to what he called "the spirit of business"—the right term today would be "the spirit of the budget." It is a shift from a concern with the creation of wealth-producing resources toward immediate payoffs. It is a shift in cost-effectiveness from emphasis on effectiveness to emphasis on cost. And this trend is perhaps a good deal more pronounced in government today than it is in business.

## Estrangement

Let us now look at what has happened to change the mood, the mind-set, the values of American science. Those changes, or at least their underlying causes, go back to an earlier period during which the relation between science and its non-scientific patrons and customers both in industry and in government seemed to be closest, most harmonious, and most productive.

American science first began to feel uncomfortable in the traditional relationship of mutually advantageous coexistence. Or perhaps science was uncomfortable all along, but did not see any alternative until after World War II, when government emerged as its rich and more generous patron. Whereas industry had at best spent hundreds of thousands and hired a dozen scientists, the government spent billions and seemed to have an insatiable appetite for well-paid science professionals in an ever-increasing number of government agencies.

Even more appealing: government increasingly offered scientists, including a great many junior ones still at the beginning of their scientific careers, the best of both worlds—to live in academia on a Washington income. No wonder that grants-manship rapidly became the most prized and the most accomplished of the liberal arts. And where industry, whenever it offered support, had the insulting habit of expecting results, government, or so it seemed, was willing to support the scientist for science's sake. Indeed anyone who in the palmy days of the early 1960s raised such nasty questions as the accountability of grants-receiving scientists for performance and results, risked being branded an anti-intellectual. And anyone who then doubted that government support would continue to grow, let alone whether government's intentions were truly honorable, was likely to be dismissed as an old fogy.

As a consequence, science became accustomed to large sums of public money, in return for which it then had to accept political rather than economic yardsticks for success and performance, the main yardstick being whether a program for the support of this or that major scientific enterprise could be sold to the governmental policy makers; and—a logical consequence—whether this or that search for knowledge fitted the political ideologies and popular fads of this or that clique or faction. Thus American science, quite understandably, came to consider the question of economic application and economic benefits to be irrelevant and irksome, if not somewhat demeaning. Few raised the question whether political favor and acclaim might not be equally irrelevant and perhaps even more demeaning as yardsticks of scientific achievement.

But I would consider even more crucial in the estrangement from industry on the part of science the fact that, for the last quarter century, work in graduate school has come to focus on the production of Ph.D.s, certified for teaching in institutions of higher learning. Prior to World War II, science teaching in the university focused on undergraduates, on students who were unlikely to make science their career. In graduate school, the focus was largely on the preparation of research scientists for outside laboratories, that is, in industry and, to a lesser extent, in government. The best graduates were the ones who then got the good jobs in industry; other jobs for graduate scientists were exceedingly scarce.

The "educational explosion" of the mid-1950s, of necessity, meant a shift in focus to basic theory, which is what an undergraduate teacher teaches. It meant, of necessity, a loss of close contact with industry. For one's brightest graduates no longer went into industry—and it is largely through his graduates that the university scientist stays in contact with the world outside of science. Indeed, the distinguished scientist's best students did not even go into undergraduate teaching, but stayed on in graduate teaching and graduate research. The educational explosion made the scholar into a mass producer, an industrialist who produced graduates. Graduate school became a growth industry, and the university largely became a closed system, preparing people for its own continuation and perpetuation.

This also changed the meaning of research. Research now became something for which one gets entitlement to a specific type of job, to promotion, or to tenure. It became a ticket of admission. Whenever a piece of work becomes a ticket of admission, it becomes increasingly formalized. It increasingly focuses on satisfying requirements rather than on producing results.

Again, fifteen years ago only an "old fogy" would have dared to suggest that graduate school enrollment and, especially, enrollment in graduate programs preparing for teaching in graduate school would not and could not expand indefinitely. Long after the "baby bust" of 1960–61 had occurred—indeed long after it had clearly become irreversible—graduate schools, and especially those in science, continued to intensify their efforts to produce larger numbers of graduates trained and mentally prepared for rapid careers in the academic "growth industry" of the ever-expanding university. When the university stopped expanding, these graduates then understandably felt let down. They did not blame the university which had led them on and had overpromised. They did not accept the facts of baby boom and baby bust. They tended to blame the outside world, namely, industry and government.

These developments may account for what, to the outside viewer, seems to be the most fundamental shift of all. This is the shift toward a definition of knowledge as "whatever has no utility and is unlikely to be applied." This is not a form of Marxism, let alone social responsibility. It is incompatible with any philosophy of society or economy. And it is far more elitist, and in the worst possible way, than the so-called elitism of the traditional scholar. It is a view of science as existing primarily for the sake of academia.

The American scientist, by and large, still invokes Francis Bacon as his patron saint. But to an outside observer, and especially an outside observer located in the employing institutions other than the university itself—that is, in government or industry—it sometimes seems that American science is rapidly shifting to its own neo-scholasticism, its own closed system. Like any scholasticism, it suspects experience, despite its emphasis on experiments. It tends to reject utility, application, technology, and any kind of payoff altogether. To the outside observer it looks as if the mind-set and the values of American science are becoming incompatible with, or at least alien to, application, utility, and results.

## The Dangers

The drift of science and industry from mutual respect and advantageous interdependence to the antagonism and alienation which characterize the last ten or fifteen years is dangerous first to American industry. The great danger is that what I have called "the spirit of the budget" will paralyze the ability to innovate and to change.

We know very little about the actual relation between scientific knowledge and technology, but we do know that science creates both vision and performance-capacity. It would be a very poor trade-off to exchange the increased analytical capacity of the policy maker in government and business for lack of vision, lack of will to innovate, and paralysis of the capacity to change. We face a period in which ability to change will be crucial—with the impacts of twentieth-century science on our vision, as well as on our technology and our way of life, just beginning to be significant.

The danger of the drift into antagonism and alienation is, however, even greater for science than it is for industry. It is possible, and even fairly easy, to buy the application of science. By its very nature, science is public. Technology, the application of science, is usually available in prepackaged and applicable form and for a reasonable fee. This has been proved by such totally different countries as the Soviet Union and Japan. In both, investment in science has been kept low—in the Soviet Union it has essentially been focused on a few selected areas considered of prime importance for defense; and in Japan it has been reserved for areas that were considered intellectually prestigious. In both countries, the technological fruits of science were readily available by purchase from the outside world.

It is not true, in other words, that a modern developed country needs a science base. It can purchase it or import it. If American science loses the support of industry and of government policy makers because it spurns both in the name of scientific "purity," it may find that for long years to come the country can get along without it. Ultimately there may be a very high price to pay—but this may well be far into the future.

In purely opportunistic terms, American science can therefore ill afford to be estranged from industry. Clearly the expectation that government would turn out to be a more reliable, let alone a less demanding, patron than industry can no longer be maintained. Government may turn out to be a far less dependable and a far more restrictive patron than the economic sector would ever be. Certainly, government is likely to impose political values on science, far more than pluralistic and atomized industry would ever do, whether this is in respect to biomedical research with its politically popular fads and crash programs, in respect to the demand that scientific research be focused on projects rather than on knowledge, or in the demand that what is science is what elects politicians or what pleases an intellectual mob.

Equally, it is no longer able to anchor American science in the graduate training of Ph.D.s for college or university teaching. Colleges and universities will for long years to come be amply staffed, especially in traditional scientific disciplines. At the same time, government employment for scientifically trained people has reached a plateau, and may indeed go down rather than up—both because the pipelines are full and because spending cuts are likely to fall on areas of long-term promise (that is, on areas that employ scientists in large numbers) rather than on areas of immediate performance.

For the next twenty-five years or so, American science will therefore have to look to industry to find employment for its graduates. It will again, as it was forty or fifty years ago, become the rule to expect one's ablest graduates to find employment and livelihood in industry. The alternative is a sharp curtailment of the academic establishment in science, and especially of graduate work in science, and almost certainly a drop in standards and quality.

## The Philosophical Issue

Modern free society rests on three foundations: autonomous local government as opposed to the centralized bureaucracy of enlightened absolutism; the autonomy of science as independent value and self-directed intellectual inquiry; and pluralism in the economic sphere, in which autonomous self-governing institutions in the pursuit of their own mission promote economic well-being. The three are interdependent.

Of the three, industry has shown itself capable of survival even if free society is snuffed out. In the most totalitarian society, the economic unit—that is, the management of industry—is still autonomous. Whenever a modern tyrant tried to subordinate the economic institutions to the all-powerful Party, he failed, and very soon. Stalin's successors learned this lesson and so today do the successors of Mao in China.

Science, by contrast, has proved to be fragile, easily subordinated to tyranny, subject to dogmatic thought control and easily swallowed up in the bureaucratic apparatus of a totalitarian system. Science, in other words, has a greater stake in the survival of an autonomous and self-governing industry than industry has in the survival of an autonomous and self-governing science.

The deterioration in the science/industry relationship may be only a symptom of far more profound changes in world view way below the surface. But the change is in itself a dangerous, a disturbing, a painful symptom that deserves being treated.

Most needed perhaps is an attitude of responsibility on the part of science. It is no longer permissible for scientists to dismiss the difficult question of the results the laity might expect from scientific endeavor and research. To say, as scientists are wont to do, that scientific knowledge is its own result beyond appraisal or measurement, could be justified when science was a marginal activity. For this is an argument with which one justifies a small luxury, or a harmless self-indulgence. We may never be able to measure scientific results, let alone to plan them. But science may—and should—be able to tell us what to expect, what to anticipate, and how to judge. Science is unlikely to be measurable. But it might hold itself accountable.

Such a change in attitude may not cure anything. But it would enable science, industry, and government to function better and more productively. And the initiative clearly rests with science. We may never be able to work out the complex relationship between science, technology, and innovation—whether in the economy, in education, or in health care. But that the scientist has a stake in the relationship and in its productivity needs to be emphasized—and most by the scientist.

But industry and the decision makers in government also need to change their attitudes and correct their vision. They know that slighting research and long-term work is dangerous and may even be suicidal. The means to convert this knowledge into action is systematic abandonment of the obsolete, the outworn, the no longer productive. In a few businesses this is understood. There every product, every technology, every process is considered as becoming obsolete, the only question being, "How fast?" And then an attempt is made to assess the amount of the new, and especially of the new science and technology that is needed to fill the gap, accepting that of every three major innovative thrusts, one at the most is likely to live up to its promise. For most businesses, however, this is still something only talked about—if not something stoutly resisted as a threat. Most businesses—and practically all governments—seem to believe that yesterday should last forever.

The traditional relation between science and its customers in the economic and governmental system was based on mutual respect and understanding and a keen awareness of interdependence. American science must effect a return to these values however old-fashioned they now appear to be.

# How to Guarantee
# Non-performance

I

NO ONE CAN GUARANTEE the performance of a public service program. But we know how to ensure non-performance with absolute certainty. Commit any two of the following common sins of public administration, and non-performance will inevitably follow. Indeed, to commit all six, as a good many public service agencies do, is quite unnecessary and overkill.

1. The first thing to do to make sure that a program will not have results is to have a lofty objective—"health care," for instance, or "to aid the disadvantaged." Such sentiments belong in the preamble. They explain why a specific program or agency is being initiated rather than what the program or agency is meant to accomplish.* To use such statements as "objectives" thus makes sure that no effective work will be done. For work is always

---

First published in *Public Administration Review*, March–April 1980.
*On this, see also "What Results Should You Expect?"

specific, always mundane, always focused. Yet without work there is non-performance.

To have a chance at performance, a program needs clear targets, the attainment of which can be measured, appraised, or at least judged. "Health care" is not even a pious intention, it indeed is at best a vague slogan. Even "the best medical care for the sick," the objective of many hospitals in the British National Health Service, is not operational. But it is meaningful to say: "It is our aim to make sure that no patient coming into Emergency will go for more than three minutes without being seen by a qualified Triage nurse." It is a proper goal to say: "Within three years, our maternity ward is going to be run on a 'zero defects' basis, which means that there will be no 'surprises' in the Delivery Room and there will not be one case of postpartum puerperal fever on Maternity." "Promoting the welfare of the American farmer" is electioneering. "Installing electricity in at least 25 percent of America's farms within the next three years"—the first goal of the New Deal's Rural Electrification Administration (perhaps the most successful public service agency in all our administrative history)—was specific, measurable, attainable, and attained. It immediately degenerated into work, and very shortly thereafter into performance.

2. The second strategy guaranteed to produce non-performance is to try to do several things at once. It is to refuse to establish priorities and to stick to them. Splintering of efforts guarantees non-results. Yet without concentration on a priority, efforts will be splintered. And the more massive the program is, the more will splintering efforts produce non-performance. But even poorly conceived programs might have results if priorities are set and efforts concentrated.

It is popular nowadays to blame the failure of so many of the programs of Lyndon Johnson's "War on Poverty" on shaky theoretical foundations. But whether poorly conceived or not, quite a few of the "Headstart" schools had significant results;

every one of them, without exception, was a school that decided on one overriding priority: having the children learn to read letters and numbers, for instance. Every one then stuck to the priority commitment, despite heavy flak from Washington and from all kinds of dogmatists.

An even more impressive example is the Tennessee Valley Authority (TVA) in the thirties. The bill establishing the TVA only passed Congress despite tremendous opposition because its backers promised a dozen different, if not incompatible, benefits to a dozen different and mutually antagonistic constituencies: cheap power, cheap fertilizer, flood control, irrigation, navigation, community development, and whatnot. TVA's first administrator, Arthur Morgan, a great engineer, then attempted to live up to these promises and to satisfy every one of his constituencies. The only result was an uncontrollably growing bureaucracy, uncontrollably growing expenditures, and total lack of any performance. Indeed, the TVA in its early years resembled nothing as much as one of those "messes" which we now attack in Washington. Then President Roosevelt removed Morgan and put in a totally unknown young Wisconsin utilities lawyer, David Lilienthal, who immediately—against all advice from all the "pros"—announced his priority: power production. And within a year, the TVA produced results—and Lilienthal, by the way, met no opposition, but was universally acclaimed as a saviour.

3. The third deadly sin of the public administrator is to believe that "fat is beautiful." But mass does not do work; brains and muscles do. In fact, overweight inhibits work; and gross overweight totally immobilizes.

One hears a great deal today about the fallacy of "throwing money at problems." But this is not really what we have been doing. We have been throwing manpower at problems, with Vietnam perhaps the worst example. And it is even worse to overstaff than to overfund. Today's administrators, whether civilian or military, tend to believe that the best way to tackle a problem is to deploy more and more people against it. But the one certain result of having more bodies is greater difficulties in logistics, in personnel management, in communications. Mass increases weight, but not necessarily competence. That requires direction, decision, strategy, rather than manpower. Overstaffing is not only much harder to correct than understaffing. It makes non-performance practically certain. For overstaffing always focuses energies on the inside, on "administration" rather than on "results," on the machinery rather than its purpose. It always leads to meetings and memoranda becoming ends in themselves. It immobilizes behind a facade of furious busyness. Harold Ickes, FDR's Secretary of the Interior and one of the New Deal's most accomplished administrators, always asked: "What is the fewest number of people we need to accomplish this purpose?" It is a long time since anyone in Washington (or in the state governments) has asked that question.

4. "Don't experiment, be dogmatic" is the next—and the next most common—of the administrator's deadly sins. "Whatever you do, do it on a grand scale at the first try. Otherwise, God forbid, you might learn how to do it differently." In technical or product innovation, we sometimes skip the pilot-plant stage, usually to our sorrow, but at least we build a model and put it through wind tunnel tests. In public service increasingly we start out with a "position," that is, with a totally untested theory, and go from it immediately to national, if not international, application. The most blatant example may have been the ultra-scholastic dogmatism with which we rushed into national programs in the "War on Poverty" that were based on totally speculative, totally untried social science theories, and backed by not one shred of empirical evidence.

But even if the theories on which a program is based are themselves sound, successful application always demands adaptation, cutting, fitting, trying, balancing. It always demands testing against reality before there is final total commitment.

Above all, any new program, no matter how well conceived, will run into the unexpected, whether unexpected "problems" or unexpected "successes." And then people are needed who truly understand because they have been through a similar program on a smaller scale, people who know whether the unexpected problem is relevant or not, but also whether the unexpected success is a fluke or genuine achievement.

Surely one of the main reasons for the success of so many of the New Deal programs was that there had been "small-scale" experiments in states and cities earlier—in Wisconsin, for instance, in New York State, or in New York City, or in one of the reform administrations in Chicago. And the outstanding administrators of the New Deal program—Frances Perkins at Labor, Harold Ickes at Interior or Arthur Altmeyer at Social Security—were all graduates of such earlier small-scale experiments. But the truly unsuccessful New Deal programs, the WPA for instance, were without exception programs that had not first been developed in small-scale experimentation in state or local governments but were initiated as comprehensive, national panaceas.

5. "Make sure that you will not learn from experience" is the next prescription for non-performance in public administration, the next one of its deadly sins. "Do not think through in advance what you expect; do not then feed back from results to expectations so as to find out what you can do well, but also what your weaknesses, your limitations, and your blind spots are."

Every organization, like every individual, does certain things well. They are the things that "come easy to one's hand." But every organization, like every individual, is also prone to typical mistakes, has typical limitations and its own blind spots. Unless the organization builds in feedback from results on its own expectations, it will not find out what it does well and thus not learn to apply its strengths. And it will also not find out what it does poorly and will thus have no opportunity to improve and to compensate for its weaknesses, its blind spots. Typically, for instance, certain institutions expect results much too fast and throw in the towel much too soon. A good many of the "War on Poverty" agencies did just that. But also, there are many organizations which wait much too long before they face up to the fact that a program or a policy is unsuccessful—our Vietnam policies, both civilian and military, probably belong here. One can only learn by feedback. And we know that feedback from results always improves performance capacity and effectiveness. Without it, however, the weaknesses, the limitations, the blind spots increasingly dominate. Without learning from results through feedback, any organization, like any individual, must inevitably deteriorate in its capacity to perform. Yet in most public service institutions such feedback from results is taboo. Or rather, if the results do not conform to expectations, they are being dismissed as irrelevant. Or they are seen as indications of the obtuseness of clients, the reactionary obscurantism of the public or, worst of all, as evidence of the need to "make another study." Most public service institutions, governmental ones as well as non-governmental ones, are budget-focused. But the budget measures efforts rather than results. For performance, the budget needs to be paralleled with a statement of expected results, and with systematic feedback from results, on expenditures and on efforts. Otherwise, the agency will, almost immediately, channel more and more of its efforts toward non-results and will become the prisoner of its limitations, its weaknesses, and its blind spots rather than the beneficiary of its own strengths.

6. The last of the administrator's deadly sins is the most damning and the most common: the inability to abandon. It alone guarantees non-performance, and within a fairly short time.

Traditional political theory, the theory inherited from Aristotle, holds that the tasks of government are grounded in the nature of civil society and thus immutable: defense, justice, law, and order. But very few of the tasks of modern public administration, whether governmental or non-governmental public service institutions—such as the hospital, the Red Cross, the university, or the Boy Scouts—are of that nature. Almost all of them are manmade, rather than grounded in the basic essentials of society. And most of them are of very recent origin, to boot. They all, therefore, have in common that they must become pointless fairly fast. They may become pointless because the need to which they address themselves no longer exists or is no longer urgent. They may become pointless because the old need appears in such a new guise as to make obsolete present design, shape, concerns, and policies. The great environmental problem of 1910, for instance—and it was a very real danger—was the horrendous pollution by the horse, with its stench, and its liquid and solid wastes, which threatened to bury the cities of that time. If we had been as environmentally conscious then as we are now, we would have saddled ourselves with agencies which only ten years later would have become totally pointless and yet, predictably, ten years later would have redoubled their efforts, since they would have totally lost sight of their objectives. But also, a program may become pointless when it fails to produce results despite all efforts, as do our present American welfare programs. And finally, most dangerous of them all, a program becomes pointless when it achieves its objectives. That we have a "welfare mess" today is, in large measure, a result of our having maintained the welfare programs of the New Deal after they had achieved their objectives around 1940 or 1941. These programs were designed to tackle the problems caused by the temporary unemployment of experienced (and almost entirely white) male heads of families—no wonder that they then mal-performed when applied to the totally different problems that were caused ten or fifteen years later by the mass movement of black females without skills or work experience from rural poverty into city slums.

The basic assumption of public service institutions, governmental or non-governmental ones alike, is immortality. It is a foolish assumption. It dooms the organization and its programs to non-performance and non-results. The only rational assumption is that any public service program will sooner or later—and usually sooner—outlive its usefulness, at least in its present form, in respect to its present objectives, and with its present policies. A public service program that does not conduct itself in contemplation of its own mortality becomes incapable of performance. In its original guise it cannot produce results any longer; the objectives have either ceased to matter, have proven unobtainable, or have been attained. Indeed, the more successful a public service agency is, the sooner will it work itself out of the job. And then it can only become an impediment to performance if it refuses to abandon. The "March of Dimes," which refused to liquidate itself after it had brilliantly accomplished the feat of conquering polio for which it had been organized, and which then became just another money-waster, is only one example.

The public service administrator who wants results and performance will thus increasingly have to build into his own organization an organized process for abandonment. He will have to learn to ask every few years: "If we did not do this already, would we now—knowing what we know now—go into it?" And if the answer is No, he better not say: "Let's make another study," or: "Let's ask for a bigger budget." He should ask: "How can we get out of this?" or at least: "How can we stop pouring more effort, more resources, more people into this?"

II

Avoidance of these six "deadly sins" does not, perhaps, guarantee performance and results in the public service organization. But avoiding these six deadly sins is the prerequisite for performance and results. And there is nothing very recondite about these dos and don'ts. They are simple, elementary, indeed obvious. Yet, as everyone in public administration knows, most administrators commit most of these "sins" all the time and indeed all of them most of the time.

One reason is plain cowardice. It is "risky" to spell out attainable, concrete, measurable goals—or so the popular wisdom goes. It is also mundane, pedestrian, and likely to "turn off" backers or donors. "The world's best medical care" is so much more "sexy" than "Every emergency patient will be seen by a qualified Triage nurse within three minutes." And to set priorities seems even more dangerous—one risks the wrath of the people who do not really care for electric power or fertilizer, but want to protect the Little Snail Darter or the Spotted Lousewort. And of course you do not "rank" in the bureaucracy unless you spend a billion dollars and employ an army of clerks.

Perhaps so—but experience does not bear out the common wisdom. The public service administrators who face up to goal-setting, to priorities, and to concentrating their resources; the public-service administrators who are willing to ask: "What is the smallest number of people we need to attain our objectives?" may not always be popular. But they are respected—and they rarely have any trouble at all. They may not get as far in their political careers as the ones who put popularity above performance—but in the end they are the ones we remember.


III


But perhaps even more important than cowardice as an explanation for the tendency of so much of public administration today to commit itself to policies that can only result in non-performance, is the lack of concern with performance in public administration theory.

For a century, from the Civil War to 1960 or so, the performance of public service institutions and programs was taken for granted in the United States. And it could be taken for granted because earlier administrators somehow knew not to commit the "deadly sins" I have outlined here. As a result, the discipline of Public Administration—a peculiarly American discipline, by the way— saw no reason to concern itself with performance. It was not a problem. It focused instead on the political process, that is, on how programs come into being. *Who Gets What, When, How?*, the title of Harold Lasswell's 1936 classic on politics, neatly sums up one specific focus of American public administration, with its challenge to traditional political theory. The other focus was procedural: "The orderly conduct of the business of government," an earlier generation called it. It was a necessary concern in an America that had little or no administrative tradition and experience and was suddenly projected into very large public service programs, first in World War I, then in the New Deal, and finally in World War II. We needed work on all phases of what we now call "management": personnel, budgeting, organization, and so on. But these are inside concerns. Now we need hard, systematic work on making public service institutions perform.

Since 1960, that is, for the last twenty years, malperformance is increasingly being taken for granted. Great programs are still being proposed, are still being debated, and, in some instances, are even still being enacted. But few people expect them to produce results. All we really expect now, whether from a new Department of Education in Washington or from a reorganization of the state government by a new governor who preaches that "Small is beautiful," is more expenditure, a bigger budget, and more ineffectual bureaucracy.

The malperformance of public service institutions may well be a symptom only—the cause may be far more basic: a crisis in the very foundations and assumptions on which rests that proudest achievement of the Modern Age, national administrative government.

But surely the malperformance of the public service institution is in itself a contributing factor to the sickness of government, and a pretty big one. Avoiding the "deadly sins" of public administration may only give symptomatic relief for whatever ails modern government. But at least we know how to do it.

# CHAPTER ELEVEN

# Behind Japan's Success

"I AM MORE AFRAID OF THE JAPANESE than I am of
the Russians, " a young lawyer, partner in a leading law firm, said
recently to me. "To be sure, the Russians are out to conquer the
world. But their unity is imposed from the top and is unlikely to
survive a challenge. The Japanese too are out to conquer us, and
their unity comes from within. They act as one superconglomer-
ate." But this is myth rather than reality. The Japanese indeed have
learned how to act in the world economy effectively and with
national consensus behind their policies. But their unity is not the
result of a "Japan Inc.," of a monolith of thought and action. It is
the result of something far more interesting and perhaps far more
important: of policies aimed at using conflict, diversity, dissent to
produce effective policy and effective action.

To any Japanese, "Japan Inc." is a joke, and not a very funny one.
He sees only cracks and not, as the foreigner does, a "monolith."
What he experiences in his daily life and work are tensions, pressures, and conflicts rather than "harmony." There is, for instance,
the intense, if not cutthroat competition between the major banks
and between the major industrial groups. And almost every Japanese

First published in *Harvard Business Review*, January–February 1981.

is himself involved personally every day in the bitter factional infighting which—rather than unity and cooperation—characterizes Japanese institutions: the unremitting guerilla warfare which each ministry wages against all other ministries; the factional sniping and bickering within the political parties and within the Cabinet, but also within each business and each university. Where the foreigner sees close cooperation between government and business, the Japanese businessman sees government attempts to meddle and to dictate, and a constant tug-of-war. "To be sure," the chief executive officer of a big company remarks, "we pull at the same rope, but we pull in opposite directions." Nor is government always successful in making industry work together and subordinate itself to what government sees as the national interest. Despite twenty years of continuous pressure, the supposedly all-powerful Ministry of International Trade and Industry (MITI) has, for instance, not gotten the major Japanese computer manufacturers to pool their efforts—something that Germany, France, and Britain have all accomplished.

One foreigner after another extols Japan's uniquely harmonious industrial relations. But the Japanese public curses at the all-too-common wildcat strikes on the government-owned National Railways. It is only where the labor unions are exceedingly weak, that is, in the private sector, that labor relations are harmonious. There is no sign of "harmony" in the public sector, where (a legacy of the U.S. occupation) unions are strong. Indeed, Japanese labor leaders are inclined to point out, somewhat acidly, that Western firms without unions—IBM, for instance—tend to have exactly the same labor policies and the same "harmony" as "Japan Inc.," so that the Japanese situation signifies management's hostility to unions rather than the fabled "harmony."

And yet—while "Japan Inc." may be more myth than reality, Japan has developed habits of political behavior which make it singularly effective as a nation in economic policy and in international economic competition. One of these habits is thorough consideration of a proposed policy's impact on the productivity of Japanese industry, on Japan's competitive strength in the world markets, and on Japan's balances of payment and of trade. This has become almost second nature with Japanese policy makers, whether in the ministries, in the Diet, or in business, and equally with analysts and critics in the popular newspapers or the university economics departments. The Japanese are far too conscious of their dependence on imports for the bulk of their energy and of their raw materials and for two fifths of their food to shrug off the external world or to push it out of their field of vision altogether, as American lawmakers, American government departments, and so many American economists are wont to do.

The Japanese do not go in for formal "productivity impact statements." And its impact on competitive position and productivity is by no means the sole criterion in adopting or rejecting a proposed policy. Even if the most powerful government agency opposes a policy because of its deleterious impacts on Japan's position in the world economy, the Japanese public or Japanese industry may yet embrace it—as they did in respect to the expansion of the Japanese automobile industry.

MITI, the powerful Ministry of International Trade and Industry has, since 1960 or 1961, steadily opposed expansion of the automobile industry—in large part because it views the private automobile as "self-indulgence" and as the opening wedge of the "consumer society" which a puritanical MITI abhors. There was also, at least in the early years, considerable skepticism about the ability of untried Japanese automobile manufacturers to compete against the likes of GM, Ford, Fiat, and Volkswagen. And there was, and is, great fear that a large automobile market in Japan will provoke irresistible demands to open Japan to foreign imports—the one thing MITI is determined to prevent. But MITI also held—and quite sincerely—that expansion of the automobile industry would have an adverse, indeed a deleterious, effect on Japan's balance of trade, on its ability to earn its way in the world economy, and on its productivity altogether. The more successful the Japanese automobile industry, MITI economists argued, the worse the impacts on Japan. The automobile, they pointed out, requires the two raw materials that are in shortest supply in Japan: petroleum and iron ore. It also requires diversion of scarce resources, both of food-growing land and of capital, to highways and highway construction. What MITI wanted was massive investment to upgrade the railroads' freight-handling capacity.

There are plenty of diehards around—and not only at MITI—who still maintain that to let the Japanese automobile industry expand was a serious mistake. The industry's export earnings, the diehards will argue, are only a fraction of what the automobile costs Japan in foreign exchange for petroleum and iron ore imports, even with record automobile sales to North America and western Europe. A small part of the sums spent on highways would have given the Japanese railroads the freight-carrying capacity which the country needs and still lacks. Yet, though enormous amounts have been spent on roads, it has not been nearly enough to build an adequate highway system—thus resulting in trucks clogging the inadequate roads, in high transportation costs for Japanese industry, in unhealthy concentration of people and factories around a few already overcrowded port cities such as Tokyo, Yokohama, Nagoya, Osaka, and Fukuoka, and in growing air pollution.

MITI lost its fight against the automobile, despite its reputation as a kind of economic superman. It was defeated in part by the automobile industry, which forged ahead despite MITI's disapproval. In large part MITI was defeated by the infatuation of "Nabe-san," the Japanese "man in the street" (and of his wife) with the motor car, despite its high costs, despite the lack of places to park, despite the traffic jams which make commuting a nightmare in every Japanese city, and despite air pollution, about which no one complains louder than "Nabe-san," sitting in the driver's seat.

But at least—and this is the point—the automobile's impact on Japan's productivity, competitive position, and balance of trade was seriously considered. And even the automobile company executives who fought MITI the hardest admit that it was the ministry's duty to make sure that these impacts were taken seriously, no matter how popular "wheels" are with the Japanese consumer and voter.

The impact on Japan's competitive position in the world economy is only one of the considerations Japanese leaders are expected to think through and weigh carefully before espousing a policy or taking a course of action. They are expected altogether to start out with the question: "What is good for the country?" rather than the question: "What is good for us, our institution, our members and constituents?"

In no other country are interest groups so well organized as in Japan, with its endless array of economic federations, industry associations, professional societies, trade groups, special interest "clubs," guilds, and what-have-you. Each of these groups lobbies brazenly and openly uses its voting power and its money to advance its own selfish ends in ways that would have made a Tammany boss blush. Yet if it wants to be listened to and to have influence on the policy-making process, every group must start out in its thinking and in its deliberations with the national interest rather than with its own concerns. It is not expected to be "unselfish" and to advocate policies that might cost it money, power, or votes—Japan's Confucian tradition rather distrusts self-sacrifice as unnatural. But the group is expected to fit what serves self-interest into a framework of national needs, national goals, national aspirations and values. Sometimes this is blatant hypocrisy, as when the Japanese physicians claim that the only thought behind their successful demand for near-total exemption from taxes is concern for the nation's health. Still, the physicians pay lip service to the rule which demands that the question, "What is the national interest?" be asked first. That it fails to do even that and instead is forced by the very logic of trade unionism to assert that "What is good for labor is ipso facto good for the country," is probably largely responsible for the Japanese union's lack of political influence and public acceptance, despite the unions' impressive numbers. And that, conversely, business management in Japan—or at least a substantial minority among business leaders—has for a hundred years subscribed to the rule that the national interest comes first, that indeed the rule was first formulated by one of the earliest of modern Japanese business leaders, the nineteenth-century entrepreneur, banker, and business philosopher Eiichi Shibuzawa (1840–1931), may also explain why business management is respectfully listened to whenever it discusses economic and social policies, even by the two fifths of the Japanese population who faithfully vote every time for avowedly Marxist and stridently anti-business parties and candidates.

The demand that they take responsibility for thinking through the policies which the national interest requires forces the leadership groups—and especially the business leaders—to lead. It demands that they take the initiative and formulate, propound, and advocate national policies *before* they become issues. Indeed, it forces the leadership groups to define what the proper issues are and should be.

In the West, and especially in the United States, the "interests"— such as the conventional "interests" in the economic sphere: business, labor, and the farmer—are expected to start out with their own concerns and their own needs and wants. This then means as a rule that they can rarely act at all in any matter that is general rather than sectional. They can only react. They cannot lead; they can only oppose what someone else proposes. For whenever a matter of general concern comes up, someone within the group is bound to fear being harmed, someone else will be opposed to doing anything at all, and a third will drag his feet. In Japan too, of course, any proposal is likely to run into opposition within any group. But the special interests and concerns of the members of the group which form the starting point for policy deliberations in the West are pushed aside in Japan until the national interest has been thought through. In the West, the individual, sectional, specific interests and concerns are the focus; in Japan, they are the qualifiers.

The Western approach tends to lead to inaction—or to "another study"—until someone from the outside proposes a law or a regulation that can then be fought as "unacceptable." But this is only rearguard action to prevent defeat or to contain damage and, even worse, the other side then determines what the issues are or should be. Yet, as the Japanese see clearly, to define the issue is the first duty of a leader.

But the Japanese approach also means that business—and the other leadership groups in society—are rarely "surprised." It is their job, after all, to anticipate and to define the issues. This does not always work, of course. Both the bureaucracy and the business leaders of Japan were totally unprepared for the explosive emergence of the environmental issue ten years ago—even though by that time it had already erupted in the United States, so that there was plenty of warning. Today the leadership groups in Japan—the bureaucracy, business, labor, and academia—prefer to ignore the challenge of women moving into professional and managerial jobs; yet the movement is gathering momentum and is grounded in irreversible demographics. But whereas in the United States business, labor, government, and academia talked of lowering the mandatory retirement age at the very time when the growing power of the older people made first California and then the U.S. Congress enact laws postponing retirement or prohibiting mandatory retirement altogether, big business in Japan anticipated the issue. And although the costs are very high, Japan's largest companies on their own and without any pressure from government, from labor, or from public opinion have raised the mandatory retirement age. "It's what the country needs," was the explanation.

The Western approach worked as long as national policy could effectively be formed through adversary proceedings and by balancing the conflicting reactions of large, well-established "blocs" or "interests"—the traditional economic policy triad of business, labor, and farmer. But with the fragmentation of politics in all Western countries where now small, single-cause zealots hold the swing vote and the balance of power, the traditional approach is clearly not adequate any longer. Thus the Japanese rule under which leadership groups, and especially those of the "interests," derive their legitimacy and authority from their taking responsibility for the national interest, and from anticipation, definition, resolution of issues ahead of time, might better serve in a pluralist society.

The third of the Japanese habits of effective behavior also originated with the banker-entrepreneur-business philosopher Eiichi Shibuzawa, in the closing years of the nineteenth century: Leaders of major groups, including business, have a duty, so Shibuzawa taught, to understand the views, behavior, assumptions, expectations, and values of all other major groups, and an equal duty to make their own views, behavior, assumptions, expectations, and values in turn known and understood. This is not "public relations" in the Western sense. It is, rather, very "private" relations—relations between individuals; relations made not by speeches, pronouncements, press releases, but by the continuous interaction of responsible men in policy-making positions.

Irving Shapiro, the chairman and CEO of DuPont de Nemours, the world's largest chemical company, was recently quoted in the American press for pointing out in a public speech that he was now being forced to devote four fifths of his time to "relations," especially with individual policy makers in the Congress and in the Washington bureaucracy, and could only spend one fifth of his time on managing his company. The only thing that would have surprised a Japanese CEO in a business of comparable importance was the one fifth Mr. Shapiro has available to run the company which he heads; very few CEOs of large Japanese companies have *any* time available for managing their companies. All their time is spent on "relations." And what time they have for the company is spent on "relations" too, rather than on "managing." They keep control through thorough and careful attention to personnel decisions in the upper ranks and through meticulous financial and planning reports. But they do not "manage"—that is left to lower levels. The top people spend their time sitting, sipping a cup of green tea, listening, asking a few questions, then sitting, sipping a cup of green tea, listening, asking a few more questions. They sit with the people from their own industry. They sit with suppliers, with the trading company people, with the managements of subsidiaries. They sit with top people from other companies in their group—as, for instance, in the famous four-hour "luncheons" in which the presidents of all companies in the Mitsubishi group come together once a week. They sit with the people from the banks. They sit with the senior bureaucrats of the various ministries, and on half a dozen committees in each of half a dozen economic and industry federations. They sit with the people of their own company in an after-hours party in a Ginza bar. They sit and sit and sit.

In these sittings they do not necessarily discuss business—and surely not their own business. Indeed, to a Westerner the conversation at times appears quite pointless. It ranges far afield—or so it seems—from issues of economic policy to personal concerns, to the other fellow's questions and his problems, to the topics of the day, to expectations for the future, and to reappraisal of lessons of the past. The aim is not to "solve" anything, but to establish mutual understanding. Then one knows where to go when there is a "problem"— and there is, of course, always one, sooner or later. Then one knows what the other person and his institution expect, can do and will do—but also what they cannot or will not do. And then, when either crisis or opportunity arrives, these immobile "sitters" suddenly act with amazing speed and decisiveness, and indeed ruthlessly. But also when the crisis comes, the others are ready to support, or equally, if they see the need, to oppose. For the purpose of all this sitting is not to like one another; not to agree with one another; not even primarily to trust one another: it is to know and understand one another and, above all, to know and understand where—and why—one does not like the other, does not agree, does not trust.

And finally, the effectiveness of the Japanese is based on their having learned that living together cannot be based on adversary relations, but must have a foundation in common interest and mutual trust.

Adversary relations in Japan have historically been fiercer, fought more violently and with less forgiveness or compassion than in the West. The popular movie *Shogun* does not exaggerate the violence of Japanese history, however much it may romanticize other aspects. Neither "Love thine enemy" nor "Turn the other cheek" is to be found in any of Japan's creeds. Even nature is violent in Japan, a country of typhoons, volcanoes, and earthquakes. Indeed, Japanese convention dictates that relations be adversary—or at least be made to appear so—where the Westerner sees no need for feuding and recrimination when, for instance, a painter or another artist of old parted company with his teacher and established his own style or school. This tradition extends today to divorce, which has reached epidemic proportions in Japan and is approaching the California rate, especially among young, educated couples. An "amicable" divorce is apparently not considered proper; it must be made to look "adversary," even if the couple parts by mutual consent and on reasonably good terms.

But all these are situations in which the relationship is dissolved for good. Where people or parties live together, let alone where they have to work together, the Japanese make sure that the relationship has at its core a mutuality of interest and a common concern. Then there can be conflict, disagreement, even combat; for then conflict, disagreement, and combat can still be confined and subsumed in a positive bond.

One of the main—though rarely voiced—reasons why the Japanese automobile companies are reluctant to build plants in the United States is their bafflement at management-union relations in the American automobile industry. They simply cannot understand them. "Our unions," said a young Toyota engineer, an avowed "leftist" and "socialist" with strong pro-union leanings, "fight management. But yours fight the company. How can they not *know* that for anything to be good for the company's employees it has to be good for the company? Where this is not taken for granted—and it's completely obvious to every one of us—no Japanese could be a manager, but no Japanese could be an employee and subordinate either."

One does not have to live and work with a competitor; hence competition tends to be ruthless between different companies in the same field and between different groups, e.g., between Sony and Panasonic or between Mitsui Bank and Fuji Bank. But whenever there has to be a continuing relationship with the opponent, common ground must be found. Then the question that always comes up first—the question indeed to which all these endless sittings and meetings between the leaders of different groups are largely devoted is: "What interests do we share?" or: "On what issues are we in agreement?" or: "What can we do together that will help both of us attain our respective goals?" And great care is then taken to avoid destruction or damage to the unity and common purpose.

Great care is also taken to see that there be no "final victory" over some group or interest with whom one has to live and work. For then to win the war means to lose the peace. Thus whenever groups or interests in Japan have to live together, both will be more concerned with making their conflict mutually productive than with winning—even though the same people in the same group will go all out for total victory and for unconditional surrender against an opponent with whom their group does not have to live and who therefore can (indeed, should) be destroyed.

These are rules and, like all rules of this kind, are ideals and normative rather than descriptive of what everybody does all the time. Every Japanese can point to dozens of cases where the rules were broken or disregarded, and with impunity. The rules are also not necessarily accepted by everybody as being right. Some of Japan's most successful entrepreneurs and business builders—Honda, for instance, or Matsushita at Panasonic, or Sony—have shown scant respect for some of them. These successful leaders do not, for example, give a great deal of time and top management attention to outside relationships, and do not care much whether they are accepted in the "club" or not. They do not necessarily agree that putting the national interest first in one's thinking and policies is the responsibility of the business leader; and they may even on occasion have been quite willing to inflict crushing defeats on opponents with whom they still have to live arid work.

There is also a good deal of criticism within Japan—especially within business—of some of the rules, and grave doubt whether they are still fully appropriate to Japan's needs. Can top management, for instance, devote practically all its time to outside relations or will it lose touch with the reality of its business at a time of rapid change in economics, markets, and technologies? And there is a good deal of grumbling to the effect that concern for finding common ground with other groups—especially for business finding common ground with government—has led to spineless appeasement and has only encouraged bureaucratic arrogance.

The rules, in other words, are similar to all other such rules in that they have weaknesses, limitations, shortcomings—and in that they do not apply universally and without exception. But they surely also have unique strengths and have been uniquely effective. What then is their essence, what is the "secret" of their success?

The most common answer, in Japan as well as in the West, is that these rules represent uniquely Japanese traditions and values. But it is surely not the whole answer, and is indeed largely the wrong answer. Of course, rules of social and political behavior are part of a culture and have to fit it, or at least be acceptable to it. And *how* the Japanese handle their policies, their rules, and their relations is very Japanese indeed. But the rules themselves represent *a* rather than *the* Japanese tradition. They represent a choice between widely different, but equally traditional, alternatives rather than historical continuity. Some of the rules, moreover, have no foundation whatever in Japanese tradition. The industrial harmony of Japan is usually attributed to history and traditional values. But the only historical tradition of relations between superior and subordinate in Japanese history is violence and open warfare. As late as the 1920s, that is, through the formative stage of modern Japanese industry, Japan had the world's worst, most disruptive and most violent labor relations of any industrial country. And for the hundred and fifty years before modern Japan was born in the Meiji Restoration of 1867, relations between "bosses" and "workers"— between the lords and their military retainers, the Samurai, who were the "bosses," and the peasants, who were the "workers"— meant at least one bloody peasant rebellion per year, more than two hundred during the period, which was then suppressed just as bloodily. "Government by assassination" rather than the building of relationships or the finding of common ground was still the rule for relationships between different groups in the 1930s. And it is not entirely coincidence that both student violence and terrorism began in Japan in the 1960s and took their most extreme form there; both are surely as much a "Japanese tradition" as the attempt to find common ground between opponents, and maybe more so.

Also these rules did not just evolve. They were strongly opposed when first propounded and considered quite unrealistic for a long time. The greatest figure in Japanese business history is not Eiichi Shibuzawa, who formulated the most important rules of behavior for today's Japanese society. It is Yataro Iwasaki (1834–85), the founder and builder of Mitsubishi, who was to nineteenth-century Japan what J. P. Morgan, Andrew Carnegie, and John D. Rockefeller, Sr., combined were to the United States. And Iwasaki rejected out of hand Shibuzawa and his rules—whether the demand that business leadership take responsibility and initiative in respect to the national interest, or the demand that it build and nurture its relationships, or in particular the idea of finding common ground with opponents and of embedding conflict in a bond of common interest and unity. Shibuzawa was greatly respected. But his teachings had little influence with "practical men," who were far more impressed by Iwasaki's business success.

Whatever their roots in Japanese traditions, these rules became accepted and the approved behavior only after World War II. Then, when a defeated, humiliated, and almost destroyed Japan began painfully to rebuild, the question was asked: "What are the right rules for a complex modern society, and one that is embedded in a competitive world economy and dependent on it?" Only then did the answers which Shibuzawa had given sixty years earlier come to be seen as right and relevant.

Why and how this happened goes well beyond the scope of this essay, and the author is hardly qualified to answer the question. There was no one single leader, no great figure, to put Japan on a new path. Indeed, the historians will be as busy trying to explain what happened in the 1950s in Japan as they have been to explain what happened at the time of Meiji, eighty years earlier, when an equally humiliated and shocked Japan organized itself to become a modern nation and yet to remain profoundly Japanese in its culture. One might perhaps speculate that the shock of total defeat and the humiliation of being occupied by foreign troops—no foreign soldier ever before had landed on Japanese soil—created a willingness to try things that had never been tried before, even though powerful forces in Japan's history had urged and advocated them. In respect to industrial relations, for instance, we know that there was no one single leader. Yet the strong need of Japanese workers, many of them homeless, many of them discharged veterans from a defeated army, many of them without employment of any kind, to find a "home" and a "community" was surely an important factor, as was the strong pressure by workers on management to protect them from the pressures of the American occupation and its "liberal" labor experts to join left-wing unions and to become a "revolutionary" force. The conservatism of the Japanese worker in the late forties and early fifties, but also the need of the Japanese worker to have a little security when his emotional, his economic, and in many cases his family ties had been severed, undoubtedly played a large part in the course Japan then took. But why Japanese management found itself able to respond to these needs and in an effective form, no one yet knows.

Indeed, the Japanese "rules" could just as well be explained with purely "Western" teachings and traditions. That business leadership, especially in big business, needs to take active responsibility and initiative for the national interest and must start out with what is good for the nation rather than what is good for business, was for instance preached in the West around 1900 by such totally un-Japanese leaders as Walter Rathenau in Germany, and Mark Hanna in the United States. That an enemy that cannot be destroyed must be made into a friend and must never be "defeated" and humiliated was first taught around 1530 by the first modern political thinker, Niccolò Machiavelli. And Japan's embedding of conflict in a core of unity is also Machiavelli—the Machiavelli of *The Discourses* rather than that of *The Prince*. Four hundred years later, in the 1920s, Mary Parker Follett, most proper of proper Bostonians, concluded again that conflicts must be made constructive by being embedded in a core of common purpose and common vision. All these Westerners—Rathenau and Hanna, Machiavelli and Follett—asked the same questions: How can a complex modern society, a pluralist society of interdependence, a society in rapid change, be effectively governed? How can it make productive its tensions and conflicts? How can it evolve unity of action out of diversity of interests, values, and institutions? And how, as Machiavelli asked, can it derive strength and cohesion from being surrounded by, and dependent on, a multitude of competing powers?

And why then did the West, and especially the United States, reject this tradition while Japan accepted it? Again the scope of this question greatly exceeds this essay and the expertise of its author. But one might speculate that the Great Depression and its trauma had something to do with it. For before it, there was indeed leadership that subscribed to these values. Both Herbert Hoover in the United States and Heinrich Bruening, the last Chancellor of a democratic Germany, represented a tradition that saw in the common interest of all groups the catalyst of national and social unity. It was their defeat by the Great Depression—for instance, in Franklin D. Roosevelt's New Deal—which ushered, in a belief in "countervailing power," in adversary relations, as leading to a compromise solution acceptable to all because it does not offend any one group too much, and therefore unites them on the least common denominator. And surely the victory of economics in the West, and especially in the United States, with their apotheosis of national government as omnipotent, omniscient, and able to control the national economy almost irrespective of what happens outside, had something to do with our forgetting the old adage of American politics that "Politics (and economic disputes) stop at the water's edge." But this is speculation.

What is fact is that the "secret" behind Japan's achievement is not a mysterious "Japan Inc.," which belongs in a Hollywood Grade B movie anyhow. It is perhaps not even the particular values of behavior that Japan has been practicing. It may be that Japan, so far alone among major industrial countries, has asked the right questions: What are the rules for a complex modern society, a society of pluralism and large organizations which have to coexist in competition and antagonism, a society that is embedded in a competitive and rapidly changing world and increasingly dependent on it?

# A View of Japan Through
# Japanese Art

JAPAN, AS EVERYBODY KNOWS, is a country of rigid rules
and of individual subordination to a collective will. It is the country
where the young college student goes hiking in the mountains, but
turns boot and pack over to a younger brother or sister upon gradu-
ation. It is the country where the student is a radical in college but
becomes a faithful conservative upon being hired by Mitsubishi Bank
or Ministry of Finance. It is the country where a young woman
wears one kind of kimono until the day of her wedding, and then
puts on the married woman's kimono for the rest of her life.

Japan is a country where junior high school graduates become
manual workers, high school graduates become clerks, and college
graduates become managers and professionals—all three thus slot-
ted for the rest of their lives by the school-leaving diploma. It is a
country where there is lifetime commitment to one employer.
Japan is also, as everyone knows, the country of mutual obligations,
in which speech is minutely regulated by social relationship and

First published in an earlier form as the concluding essay in *Song of the Brush,
Japanese Paintings from the Sansō Collection*, edit: John M. Rosenfield and Henry
Trubner (Seattle, Wash.: Seattle Art Museum, 1979).

status. It is the country of "Japan Inc.," where conflicting interests pull together for the greater glory of the common economy. The best-known—and best—book on Japanese social organization and institutions, *Japanese Society* by Chie Nakane, *depicts the *ie*, the community of the clan or tribe, as the organizing reality within which the individual exists as a member rather than as a person. Whenever Japanese and Western (especially American) scholars meet, in any discipline and on any subject, the Japanese at once contrast Japanese cooperation with the excessive competition and rampant diversity of the West.

Yet the most pervasive trait of all Japanese art is its individualism. In every major period of artistic activity in the West there has been one universal style; we speak of the Hellenistic, of the Romanesque and the Gothic, the Renaissance and the Baroque. But every period of great artistic activity in Japan has been characterized by diversity. Indeed, in the arts, and especially in painting, the contrast is properly between Western conformity and the "excessive diversity" of Japan. During the Edo period (1603–1867), the Japanese tendency to diversity reached its apogee. In painting alone, over a dozen major schools flourished, along with countless subschools. There is nothing comparable in other cultures to the flamboyant diversity of the last great artistic era of pre-modern Japan.

The Japanese scholars and experts who castigate American excessive competition, and who contrast it to its disadvantage with Japanese cooperation, think of competition among businesses in the marketplace or of competition for promotion within the management group in a company. They never, it seems, think of the Japanese school system. Yet every American recoils in horror when told that a Japanese schoolboy, ten years old, will applaud with joy upon hearing that his best friend is ill and will have to miss a week or two of school. The friend will thus fall behind in the

---

*(Berkeley: University of California Press, 1970).

competition for the examination that will decide on the few who will make it into the prestigious junior high school.

And as to "Japan Inc.," there is no commercial rivalry and competition in the West that compares with the fierce ruthlessness with which the major Japanese industrial groups, the *zaibatsu*, fight one another. If Mitsubishi goes into a new field, be it synthetic fibers or electronics or shipbuilding, Mitsui and Sumitomo have to go into it too—never mind that overcapacity already exists in that industry worldwide. And Japanese political parties are not disciplined monoliths; they are not an *ie*. They are loose congeries of fiercely competing factions.

The Japanese are probably the world's best animal painters. In the West, the few animal painters are specialists, a Rosa Bonheur or George Stubbs, for instance. In Japan almost every painter painted animals. The Japanese took some traditions of animal painting from the Chinese: the *kachōga* (flower-and-bird) painting, for instance. But most animals, and especially the birds, in Japanese painting express purely native Japanese values, traditions, and perceptions.

Nothing I know expresses one basic trait of the Japanese as well as these bird paintings do: the capacity for pure enjoyment. It is the same capacity one gets at a Japanese picnic or at a simple folk dance in an empty lot on a summer's night. It is the capacity for pure enjoyment that makes pompous company presidents and grave scholars play at the silliest children's games at a party, without embarrassment or reticence. It is the capacity for pure enjoyment that can be seen in parks on Sundays where young Japanese fathers romp with their children. It is a quality of immediacy that is present in the most sophisticated Japanese artwork or novel, and that is the essence of the *haiku*. The traditional Japanese animal or bird painting always looks ludicrously simple—just a few strokes of the brush. Yet it is done with complete control of brush, ink, and composition. It also expresses the artists' intuitive, immediate projection of their own selves into the spirit of the birds or the frog.

These Japanese paintings are a hymn to diversity and spontaneity in keeping with the first of the modern English poets, the late Victorian Gerard Manley Hopkins, who sang, "Glory be to God for dappled things."

And yet the cooperation, the mutual obligations, the lifetime commitment to one employer, the *ie*, and even "Japan Inc.," are not myths. Central to Japan is constant and continuing polarity between tight, enveloping community—supportive but demanding subordination to its rules—and competitive individualism demanding spontaneity.

Japanese artists of the eighteenth century were highly individualistic, yet most considered themselves as belonging to a school— Nanga or Rimpa or Shijō, for instance. The few who did not— Shōhaku, Rosetsu, Jakuchū—are called "eccentrics" in Japan. And if an artist starts in a school and then outgrows it and develops his own style, Japanese propriety demands that there be a violent break, like the confrontations of a Kabuki drama. Nagasawa Rosetsu (1755–99), for instance, is reported to have broken violently with Maruyama Okyo (1733–95), whose student he originally was, though the record shows unambiguously that the two actually kept on working together and that Okyo entrusted Rosetsu with important and confidential commissions. Similarly, a century earlier, Kusumi Morikage (d. before 1700) was reported to have been excommunicated by, and exiled from, the atelier of Kanō Tanyū (1602–74) when he went his own way, though the record shows a close and continuing family relationship between the two artists.

Even today, in a modern, Westernized Japan, it is not considered proper for a young man to be on his own and not to belong to an organization, an *ie*. My interpreter on my first lecture tour in Japan, more than twenty years ago, was a young Japanese who had gone to graduate school in the United States and who had then established his own marketing consulting practice in Tokyo. He was, I found out, not welcome in his father-in-law's house. When I met the father-in-law, who was dean at a university where I lectured,

I asked him what he had against his son-in-law. "He is barely thirty," he replied, "and on his own; that's quite improper. He has no organization to back him up, no boss to bail him out when he gets into trouble. What's worse, he is successful and thus sets a dangerous precedent." The point of the story is that the father-in-law was known all over Japan as the Red Dean, who delivered himself every Saturday evening on national radio of a violent philippic against the remnants of feudalism in Japanese family life and against the evils of the organization man.

Art history (or art anecdote) may provide the answer to the paradox, and a key to understanding the relationship between the rigid community of the *ie* and the spontaneity and individualism that characterize so much of Japanese art as well as of Japanese life and society. Sakai Hōitsu (1761–1828), the last of the great Rimpa masters, started out studying under a Kanō painter around 1790. He then became the pupil of a distinguished Nanga artist, Kushiro Unsen (1759–1811). Next he apparently went for career advice to Tani Bunchō (1764–1840), the recognized Nanga master in the city of Edo, Japan's political capital. Bunchō did not tell the young Hōitsu to stick to Nanga, but counseled him to study the works of Ogata Kōrin (1663–1743) and to become a Rimpa painter. A great teacher in the West might have said to such a highly gifted young man: "Find the style that fits you." Bunchō said, in effect: "Find the school that fits you."

The tension between the pressure to belong and to conform and the stress on spontaneity, independence, and individuality is one, but only one, of the polarities that characterize Japanese art and Japanese culture. The Sansō Collection contains three works by famous seventeenth-century masters; *Two Wagtails*, attributed to Kanō Sanraku (1559–1635); the *Child Holding a Spray of Flowers*, attributed to Tarawaya Sōtatsu (early seventeenth-century); and a circular fan, *Autumnal Ivy Leaves with Bamboo*, by Ogata Kōrin. Each epitomizes the Japanese talent for simplicity refined to the point of austerity. Yet Sanraku's best-known paintings, such as his screens of birds and trees and flowers, are ornate and sumptuous, with gold and silver and ostentatious colors. Sōtatsu founded the decorative Rimpa School, with its strong lyricism and colorful elegance, and Kōrin perfected it with his rich designs. Thus the three paintings in the Sansō Collection may be called atypical of their painter—and yet each is also completely typical of him.

Similarly, in the exhibition there is a landscape by the early sixteenth-century painter Kantei that simplifies and makes more austere the already simplified and austere style of the fifteenth-century Japanese landscape painter. But there is also a pair of flower-and-bird paintings by the same master that is ornate, decorative, almost sumptuous. Almost two hundred years later, in the early nineteenth century, Watanabe Kazan, the most austere of Neo-Confucians, painted a lush, sensuous, colorful picture of *Lotus Flowers and Swimming Fish*.

To a Westerner these seem to be contradictions; to a Japanese they are polarities. A Westerner may feel that an artist should be attracted either to the austerity and empty space of a fifteenth-century landscape or to the colorful, decorative design of a Kantei flower-and-bird painting or a Sanraku bird screen, but not to both. To the Japanese, however, these are necessary tensions, poles of expression within the same person.

Any visitor to Kyoto sees examples of these tensions within a few miles of each other: Nijō Castle—ornate, sensuous, boastful, the official Kyoto residence of the military dictator, the Tokugawa shogun; and Katsura Villa—simple to the point of being austere, exquisite, without ornaments, and totally disciplined, the summer villa of an imperial prince. Both were built within the same generation and by the same ruling class. And there is Nikkō, north of Tokyo, the great seventeenth-century mausoleum of the first Tokugawa shōgun Ieyasu—the "shōgun" of the movie of that name—with its extreme ornateness, almost too much, even for Baroque tastes. But the same shōgun, in his castle, lived in restrained austerity. To the Japanese, the two belong together. The tension is not one of opposites, but one of poles; and where there is a north pole there has to be a south pole.

This tension, this polarity, extends through all of Japanese culture. It is found in the tension between the official Confucian male supremacy, which dictates that in public the woman is invisible and subservient, and the reality of family life, where the woman holds the power and the purse strings, and where a recent prime minister could say in parliament: "I have no position on this measure yet; my mother-in-law has been sick and I could not get her guidance," to which the opposition spokesman nodded, replying: "Please convey my wishes for a speedy recovery to your respected mother-in-law."

A similar polarity is found in the upbringing of children. Until they reach school age, children are indulged in a way that goes beyond any American permissiveness. Then they go to school, and on the first day there is discipline and the children are expected to behave—and they do. There is a remarkable tension between the genius of the Japanese language, in which everything focuses on human relationship, and the nature of Chinese ideographs, which are built up of representations of objects. The Japanese very early invented syllabaries in which the sounds of Japanese can easily be written. Every Japanese learns the two national syllabaries in the elementary grades. But then the syllabaries are used mainly as auxiliaries to Chinese ideographs. To the Japanese, the tension between the Japanese language and the Chinese ideograph is essential, no matter how heavy a burden it puts on learning and literacy.

There are strict rules for proper behavior that tell every Japanese what form of address to use when talking to his aunt and to his uncle's boss and to his cousin's mistress. But there is also the encouragement of the eccentric, who is given almost infinite leeway. Sengai, the last and perhaps greatest of the "Zenga Expressionists"—he died in 1838, aged almost ninety—for instance, was the most respected cleric, abbot of an ancient and most sacred temple; but at the age of eighty-five he was also a free spirit, who traveled around the country, often in low company, and liked to paint satirical frogs to look like the Buddha, circus riders, and balloon vendors at county fairs.

This polarity can be found today in Japanese industry and its human relations. To a Westerner, an organization can be either autocratic or democratic, but the Japanese organization is both. Surely no more perfect example of the autocratic personality exists than the head of a big Japanese organization, whether government agency or business. Yet decision making is by consensus and participation, and starts at the bottom rather than at the top. In every Japanese organization from ancient times to the present the word of the chief has been absolute law; the chief could order a retainer to commit suicide or to divorce his wife. And yet no chief could make one step without the consent of his retainers, and indeed without active participation of the clan elders in the decision. Similarly, today the top people in a company or a government agency are obeyed without argument or reservation—and yet every decision comes up from below and is an expression of a general will. Every Japanese organization is in Western terms both an extreme of autocracy and an extreme of democratic participation.

The tension is not dialectic, and resolved in a higher synthesis, nor does one principle overcome the other. It is not the dualism of the Chinese yin and yang. The Japanese do not mix their principles any more than one mixes north pole and south pole. For the Japanese tension is not contradiction or contrast or conflict—the tensions of the analytical mind. It is polarity—the tension of perception, of configuration, of existence. To understand Japanese art and Japanese life, one has to accept the polarity between the ornate and the austere; between male supremacy and female power; between spoiled, indulged brats and disciplined scholars; between the Japanese language with its inflected verbs and syllabary script and the complexities of the Chinese ideograph. Such polarities are essential to Japan and, to my knowledge, to Japan alone.

It is this tension, this polarity, that has made Japan throughout its history a country of contrasts, of sharp and sudden swings: from wide-open receptivity to foreign cultures and foreign commerce to self-imposed isolation, for instance, in the seventeenth century. But it is also this polarity that gives Japanese art, Japanese literature, and Japanese industry their dynamics and creativity.

A Westerner who has business in Japan—the professor who goes there to lecture or the businessman who negotiates a contract— soon becomes familiar with the phrase "*Wareware Nihon-jin,*" which means "We Japanese." But whenever it is used (and it is used all the time), it conveys: "We Japanese are so different that you will never understand us." To understand what a Japanese friend or business partner, or the student in the audience who gets up and asks a question, means when he starts out with *Wareware Nihon-jin,* one needs to look at Japanese landscape paintings. But where in the landscapes are the people—the *Nihon-jin?* Yet it is precisely their absence, or their subordination to the land, that is the point. For *Nihon-jin* does not just mean Japanese. It means: "We who belong to the land of Japan." The landscape painting is the soul of Japanese art because the Japanese landscape has formed the soul of Japan.

Some of the features of these landscape paintings the Japanese took from the Chinese—the bizarre rock formation of the eroded Chinese karst limestone that can be seen in so many Japanese landscape paintings is an example. But most of the features of these landscapes can be found in Japan; indeed, a Japanese friend of mine claims that he knows the valley, someplace near Gifu, that Gyokudō, the great nineteenth-century landscape painter, so often painted in his small lyrical landscapes. The Japanese landscape looks like the landscape of the Japanese painters, as everyone knows who has traveled in the Japanese countryside. And yet the Japanese landscape does not look a bit like the landscape of the Japanese landscape painter, nor does any landscape on earth. The landscape of the Japanese painter is a spiritual landscape, a landscape of the soul.

The Japanese feeling for this landscape is part of "Shinto." What Shinto really means, probably no Westerner has ever been fully able to understand. It surely does not mean a religion in the Western sense; it became a religion only after 1867, when the Meiji Restoration created a monstrosity known as State Shinto because it felt it had to emulate the way religions are set up in the West. Far more ancient and pervasive are the many Shinto shrines and rituals, but there is, above all, a Shinto feeling—the feeling of the uniqueness of Japan as an environment. I did not write human environment; it is far more than that. It is an environment fully as much for the supernatural, for the forces that control the universe, as it is an environment for man and beast, plant and rock. It is unique and it is complete. And it is different, which is the point of *Wareware Nihonjin.* Underlying the phrase is the feeling that Japan is unique; that Japan is by itself. What this means is expressed in the landscape paintings. Their hills and trees are the visible surface, the skin, of a spiritual landscape that is invisible and unique. There may be landscapes elsewhere that look like it. Taiwan has similar hills, and so does Korea. But there is no landscape, to a Japanese, that means the same thing. A painting of the Japanese landscape can be a realistic image that serves as a valid legal document to determine the boundary lines of a Shinto shrine, as some of the earliest Japanese landscape paintings were intended to do; but even then it also means an inner space, a landscape of the soul that is the center of gravity of Japanese existence. This landscape is, so to speak, Japan *an sich.*

I am not saying that the Japanese are, in fact, unique; I am saying that the Japanese feel that they are. It is not that they feel superior; nationalism has been a Japanese vice only in rare, short moments of aberration. They feel different because they feel at home only in this landscape of their soul. This may explain why, of all the foreign students in the United States and Europe, the Japanese are the only ones, who, with few exceptions, cannot wait to go back home.

I now come to what I would call "Japanese aesthetics," or the "topological approach," or "What makes the Chinese so uneasy when they look at a Japanese painting?"

Almost any Japanese landscape painting could be used to demonstrate Japanese aesthetics. The fifteenth-century paintings deliberately set out to follow the Chinese; and so did the Nanga painters of the eighteenth century. And yet, put a Chinese connoisseur or a Chinese art historian in front of these painters' works and he will be uneasy. "Yes, these hills look like so-and-so in China. And yes, this rock looks like some other painter in China. And the brushwork is this or that school. And the brush technique, of course, follows another Chinese example. And yet, and yet, and yet . . ." What he is saying, if he is candid, is: "And yet these are definitely not Chinese paintings. They make me very uneasy and I do not understand why. But I do not want to have them around."

One only has to put these works next to Chinese paintings to understand his feelings. I am not saying that one cannot mistake a Chinese painting for a Japanese one, and vice versa. The technique is the same, the brushstrokes are the same, the ink values are the same—and the painting is different. What makes it different is the Japanese sense of beauty. The Japanese paintings are dominated by empty space. It is not only that so much of the canvas is empty. The empty space organizes the painting. This is the opposite to what most Chinese would do, but it is basic to Japanese aesthetics. The same aesthetics are found in Japanese paintings of all schools, and in the works of painters who followed the Chinese as well as in the works of painters who rejected the Chinese.

If I were to define these aesthetics in contrast to those in Western and Chinese painting, I would say that Western painting is basically geometric. It is no coincidence that modern Western painting begins with the rediscovery of linear perspective, around 1425, that is, with the subordination of space to geometry. Chinese painting, on the other hand, is algebraic. In Chinese painting, proportion governs, as it does in Chinese ethics. Japanese painting is by contrast topological—that branch of mathematics that began around 1700 and that deals with the properties of surface and space in which shapes and lines are defined by space, so that there is no difference between a straight line and a curve, such as a hyperbola. Topology deals with angles and vortices and boundary lines. It deals with what space imposes rather than with what is imposed on space. The Japanese painter is topological in his aesthetics. He sees space and then he sees lines. He does not start out with the lines.

It has been commonplace for Western art critics and art historians for almost a hundred years to say that painters do not see objects but configurations. But the *Gestalt* that the Japanese painter sees is what we today would call a design rather than a structure. This is what the topologist means when he says that, topologically speaking, it is space that determines the line rather than the line that determines space. In discussions of Japanese painting, one usually finds a reference to the Japanese tendency to become "decorative." The Nanga painters of the eighteenth century abhorred the decorative as totally incompatible with the values and aesthetics of their Chinese literati models; and yet, as we are told by all authorities, they always became decorative. Like so many words in art criticism, "decorative" is misleading; the right word might be "designed." And this irrepressible tendency toward design—the tendency that explains why ceramics, lacquer, and painting in Japanese art tend to be closely allied, while the Chinese kept them strictly separate artistically and socially—is based on a Japanese vision that is neither perspectival (i.e., geometric) nor proportional (i.e., algebraic), but topological in design.

Both the fifteenth-century black-ink painters and the eighteenth-century Nanga painters looked to the Chinese as models and masters. Both learned techniques from the Chinese, but also motives and style and form. But both transmuted Chinese algebra into Japanese topology. This ability to receive a foreign culture and then to "Japanize" it is a continuing thread in Japanese history and experience.

Around A.D. 500, Buddhism, and with it the highly advanced and most refined civilization of China, swept into Japan. At first the impact seemed to inundate Japan completely. Everything was brought from China or Korea, including monks and architects and artists and artisans and scribes and poetry and artworks and textiles. After only two centuries, by the Nara period, Japan was producing religious sculpture that was completely Buddhist and yet deeply Japanese, even though the techniques were still those of the Chinese and Korean sculptors. But Japan equally transmuted China's governmental and social structures. It made both Buddhism and Confucianism serve a tribal, and soon thereafter, a warrior society. It made Chinese concepts of land tenure, grounded in family ownership of soil, serve a system in which there was no ownership of land at all, except by temples and the throne. There were only graduated rights to the product of the land—that is, graduated rights to tax and tribute rather than ownership rights in land as such. The same thing happened in ceramics, in poetry, and in architecture.

It is happening again today; only now it is the West rather than China that is the foreign culture that is being Japanized. Forms, techniques, and concepts are used very skillfully. As the fifteenth-century and the eighteenth-century painters did, the Japanese rapidly improve on the techniques. There are few Chinese painters whose control and command of the brush equal the artistry of the great fifteenth-century Japanese landscape painter Sesshū. There are few Western companies that have the control and command of the corporate form and of managerial techniques that the large Japanese trading companies possess. But the essence is Japanese. The Japanese are not unaffected by the foreign influence; it becomes part of their own experience. Yet they distill out of the foreign influence whatever serves to maintain and strengthen Japanese values, beliefs, traditions, purposes, relationships. The result is not a hybrid. It is, as the fifteenth-century paintings or the eighteenth-century paintings show, all of one piece. This is a truly unique Japanese characteristic.

Again and again, Japanese society has lived through periods when it was wide open to foreign influences. But then it closes in again, to digest, transmute, and transform almost alchemically. What is considered base metal in the foreign culture sometimes becomes gold in Japan, as with the Chinese thirteenth-century painters Mu-ch'i or Yin T'o-lo. Both were rejected by the Chinese as "coarse" or "vulgar." They then became the models and masters for the most austerely refined Japanese painters of the fourteenth and fifteenth centuries. But sometimes the metal in a foreign culture may become dross in Japan, as happened in this century to the idea of the national state, imported from the West and transmuted into a poisonous parody of an old and peculiarly Japanese political form, the shōgunate, or military government. Always before the shōgun had served to eliminate fighting, to make war both unnecessary and impossible, and, above all, to prevent foreign adventure.

The Japanese aesthetics are a way to understand, or at least to perceive, a fundamental and central element: the very special (I would say unique) relationship between Japan and the outside world. It is a relationship based on receptivity, on an ability to learn quickly and to improve on what is being taught, while at the same time accepting, or at least retaining, only what makes Japan more Japanese: what fits topology rather than geometry or algebra; what fits Japanese human relations; what fits the inner experience of the uniqueness of Japan, and what might be called, with a Western term, Japanese spirituality. We are talking here of an existential phenomenon; and by the way, the best translation of the peculiar word "Shinto" is probably spirituality.

Whether it can maintain these abilities is the great question ahead of Japan, I think. Japan is now becoming integrated into the outside world, and not just economically (perhaps least of all economically) in a way which neither the Japan of the sixth century, that of the Buddhist and Chinese tidal wave, nor the Japan of Sesshū's time around 1500, nor perhaps even the Japan of a hundred years ago, could have imagined. Is it still possible for Japan to encapsulate and transmute into Japanness the foreign, the non-Japanese, culture, behavior, ethics and even aesthetics?

I dare not even speculate—but there are a few straws in the wind. If one looks at the visual arts that today prosper in Japan—the modern Japanese woodblock print; the Japanese movie; modern Japanese ceramics; and perhaps one could add Japanese architecture—one would say that there is a possibility, even a probability, that the Japanese are again Japanizing the imported culture. The Japanese woodblock print is modern and Japanese very much in the way in which Nara sculpture was Buddhist and Japanese. So too, to a large extent, are the ceramics of Japan today. I can hope only that the Japanese will do again what they have done before so many times. The world needs a culture that is both modern and distinctly, uniquely, non-Western. It needs a Japanese Japan rather than a Japanese version of New York or Los Angeles or Frankfurt.

"Ten minutes and eighty years," Hakuin Ekaku, the great eighteenth-century Zen master, is said to have answered when asked how long it took him to paint one of his paintings of Daruma, the founder of the Zen sect. Of course, Rembrandt might have given the same answer when asked how long it took him to paint the self-portraits of his old age, Claude Monet when asked how long it took him to paint one of the hymns to light in his versions of Rouen Cathedral, or Pablo Casals when asked how long it took him to play one of Bach's "Unaccompanied Suites for Cello." But Hakuin's answer has two levels of meaning beyond that of the Western artist: it expresses a Japanese view of the nature of man, and a Japanese view of the nature of learning.

These may be seen in the one dimension in Japanese figure and portrait painting for which the West has no real parallel, nor China either—the spiritual self-portrait. If the Westerner says that it takes eighty years to be able to do what Rembrandt's last self-portraits represent, or Monet's pure light and Casals' Bach, he talks of the decades of practice needed to attain the skill. But the "eighty years" of the Japanese saying refer, above all, to the spiritual self-realization needed to become the person who can paint Daruma. An old Zen saying has it that "Every painting of Daruma is a [spiritual] self-portrait." The Zen painter who has not worked for decades on control of the self will not be the person to paint Daruma. Daruma is not a god, he is not a saint. He is man, but one who has realized man's full spiritual potential, who has attained man's full spiritual power, and who has transformed himself into a spiritual being. And only the painter who has himself become the spiritual man which Daruma represents can then paint a portrait on which he can inscribe, as Hakuin did on one of his *Darumas*, "This Is IT!" The spiritual power, the spiritual qualities of Daruma cannot be faked. No matter how great a painter's skill, if he lacks these qualities, his *Daruma* will lack them too.

Kanō Tanyū, in the mid-seventeenth century, and Rosetsu, a century later, very great masters and without peers in painting skill, both painted Daruma. Tanyū's *Daruma* looks like an elderly bureaucrat or successful banker; Rosetsu's like the urbane and witty chairman of a university graduate department. Both are excellent paintings—but neither has spirituality, power, total compelling control. But the *Daruma* by a painter who himself has the spirituality will have that power even if, as in the case of a *Daruma* painted by Hakuin in his extreme old age, the body is weighed down by the physical infirmity of advanced old age, the eyes are almost blind despite heavy glasses, the legs have given out, and death is very near.

Daruma is mortal. He is a sentient being. But unlike the saints of Christianity or of Buddhism, he is not dependent on divine grace, on a Supreme Being, or on redemption. He had attained spiritual perfection through his own efforts and by fulfilling the divinity within him. This is not a "humanist" view of man but a spiritual and existential one. It is a view that focuses on wisdom rather than on knowledge; on self-control rather than on power; on excellence rather than on success.

The Zen saying of "ten minutes and eighty years" also expresses a uniquely Japanese concept of continuous learning. In the West and in China, one learns to prepare oneself for the next job, for a promotion, for a new challenge. The most extreme example was the Confucian examination system of Imperial China, where one actually had to unlearn what the first examination tested to get ready for the next, the second one. The Western modern medical school is not too different either, nor are most Advanced Management courses. But in Zen, one learns so as to do better what one already does well. One keeps on painting Daruma until the control becomes completely spontaneous. One draws, as did the early seventeenth-century calligrapher Konoe Nobutada, a picture of Tenjin, the patron of learning, every morning—the same picture, but with ever-increasing mastery. Or, like Nakabayashi Chikutō, around 1800, one paints the same landscapes over and over again. Of course, in the West the artist does that too—Casals practiced the Bach cello suites until his death, well past ninety years of age. But in the West—and in China—only the artist does this; the rest of us are like Confucian scholars who pass one examination to be qualified to sit for the next, and for whom one promotion is the stepping stone to the next.

In Japan there is to this day the specialist in the trading company, the specialist on cotton, for instance, or on woodworking machinery, who gets more money and a bigger title but stays the specialist on cotton or on woodworking machinery all his working life, becoming more accomplished with every year. There is the continuous learning process in the Japanese factory, where employees get more money with seniority but keep on doing the same job, and meet every week to discuss how they can do their present jobs better. And there is the uniquely Japanese concept of the Living National Treasure, the great craftsman or artist who has excelled through doing the same work. The Western theory of the learning curve is not accepted in Japan—the theory that people reach a plateau of accomplishment after a certain time and then stay on it. The Japanese learning curve has them break out of that plateau again by continuing to practice—until they reach a new plateau, when they again, after a time, start learning and growing, and so on, always approaching perfection. The Japanese learning curve, like the Zen master's ten minutes and eighty years, sees learning as an act of spiritual perfection and personal self-development as much as an acquisition of skills. It is a way of changing the person, and not just a way of acquiring performance capacity.

Again this is but one strand. Japanese history and Japanese society are as full of climbers, of ambitious schemers, of people on the make and people on the take, as any other history or society. But there is also the counterpoint—the ten minutes and eighty years of continuous learning to do better what one already does very well.

The Japanese or Zen concept of learning is not without dangers. It can degenerate into imitation and repetition. This is what happened to the Kanō School of painting. It was Japan's "official" art for almost three hundred years, from the mid-sixteenth to the mid-nineteenth century. It maintained itself in this position by insistence on continuous learning, on meticulous technique, on close adherence to the models. Thus it retained its technical competence. But it also, after 1650 or so, rapidly degenerated into mechanical copying. And it was still at mechanical copying when the Meiji Restoration opened Japan to the West more than two centuries later. But though capable of degenerating into mechanical copying and mindless repetition, the Zen tradition is closer to being a genuine theory of learning than the Western and Chinese concept of learning for the sake of advancement, promotion, or moving on. With its focus on developing the strengths of a person, it anticipated by hundreds of years modern theories of the person and of self-realization. There is indeed profound wisdom in the insight that work is an extension of personality and personality a distillation of work, so that one cannot paint Daruma's spiritual qualities without having them oneself, but so that one also becomes Daruma by painting him every day for decades.

The insight and wisdom that lie in the Zen conception of the person and of learning are endangered in today's Japan. The Japanese educational system has opted for an extreme of the Western and Confucian position, which sees the purpose of learning as getting ready for the next examination, the next promotion, the next external reward. Infants are drilled to pass the entrance examination to the right nursery school, so as to be admitted to the entrance examination to the right kindergarten, which in turn leads to the entrance examination to the right elementary school, and on to high school, the university, and the corporation. Is there still room for the emphasis on learning to become, on learning to be, on learning to say, "This is IT!" when painting *Daruma* as a spiritual portrait?

I have so far used Japanese painting to look at Japan. Now I shall use—or abuse—Japanese painting to look at the West and at Western modern art. Rosetsu painted *The Temple Bell at Dōjō-ji* in the 1780s. The title refers to a well-known Kabuki play. But the painting itself is virtually abstract and non-objective. Yet it was painted a century and a half before there were abstract painters in the West. It is by no means Japan's oldest abstract painting; in fact, such paintings can be traced back to the Heian period of the tenth century. Tani Bunchō, the great master-painter in Edo—today's Tokyo— painted a *Flowering Plum Tree in the Moonlight* shortly after 1800. It anticipates what Turner or Monet tried to do half a century later in the West: to make light the subject of a painting. A Hakuin *Daruma* is an expressionist painting, like those of Klimt, Schiele, and Kubin, and Picasso in his expressionist years, and Matisse; but with a power very few of them had. Modernism in Western art is thus anticipated by Japanese tradition. There is a story—perhaps apocryphal— that Picasso was taken in 1953 through an exhibition in Paris of Japanese paintings that featured the works of the Zen priest and painter Gibon Sengai, who had died in 1838, and that he stormed out of the exhibition exclaiming furiously that it was a hoax since no one could possibly have painted like this without first having seen his, Picasso's work. Modernism in Western art is in fact anticipated, if not prefigured, by the Japanese tradition.

Yet, of course, Westerners had never laid eyes on the Japanese originals or even heard of them. Other than *ukiyo-e*, the woodblock prints, Japanese art was virtually unknown in the West until fairly recent years. The West, in other words, has developed within the last century elements of a modern vision and sensibility that were ancient in Japan. The West has learned to see in somewhat the same way that the Japanese have seen all along. The West has shifted from description and analysis to design and configuration.

Marshall McLuhan has announced that the electronic media have changed our ways of seeing and interpreting the world, and are making us perceive rather than conceive. But a view of Western perception as informed by an understanding of Japanese art would lead to the conclusion that this shift began much earlier and owed nothing to electronic technology. On the contrary, it would appear more probable that the West became ready for the electronic technology and receptive to it because its perception had shifted from traditional description and analysis to the perception of design and configuration that Japan had known all along.

A distinguished historian of modern Western painting, Robert Rosenblum, in his recent *Modern Painting and the Northern Romantic Tradition: Friedrich to Rothko*,* asserts that modern Western painting has its roots in the northern, mostly North German, painters of the nineteenth century—Caspar David Friedrich and Otto Runge—who shifted from description to design. But this, it could be argued, is precisely what had occurred in Japan far earlier: perception as against conception, design as against description, topology as against geometry, and configuration as against analysis, have indeed been continuing characteristics of Japanese art from the tenth century on.

Edwin O. Reischauer, the former American ambassador to Japan and the foremost authority on Japanese history and society, wrote in his recent book, *The Japanese*,[†] that Japan has never produced a great or original thinker of the first rank. This has been read as severe criticism, especially in Japan; but Reischauer's point was that Japan's genius is perceptual rather than conceptual.

The towering achievement of the high Middle Ages in the West was Thomas Aquinas' *Summa Theologica*, perhaps the boldest

---

*(New York: Harper & Row, 1977).

†(Cambridge, Mass.: The Belknap Press, 1978).

conceptual and analytical feat in human history. The proudest achievement of Japan's "Middle Ages," the eleventh century, is the world's first novel, Lady Murasaki Shikibu's *Tale of Genji*, filled with intimate descriptions of men and women in court life, of love and illness and death. Japan's greatest playwright, Chikamatsu Monzaemon (1643–1724), had neither camera nor screen, but his Kabuki and Bunraku (puppet) plays are highly cinematic. They are song, dance, costumes, and music, as well as the spoken word. The characters are defined not so much by what they say as by how they appear. People rarely quote a line that Chikamatsu wrote. Yet no one ever forgets a scene. Chikamatsu was not a dramatist but a scriptwriter of genius. And without benefit of cinematic tools, his Kabuki theater invented cinema techniques; the *mie* in which the actors freeze, is, for instance, the equivalent of the movie close-up.

The perceptual in Japanese tradition largely underlies Japan's rise as a modern society and economy. It enabled the Japanese to grasp the essence, the fundamental configuration of things foreign and Western, whether an institution or a product, and then to redesign. The most important thing that can be said about Japan as viewed through its art may well be that Japan is perceptual.

# ACKNOWLEDGMENTS

Grateful acknowledgment is made for permission to reprint:

"Toward the Next Economics" originally appeared in *Public Interest*, Fall 1980.

"Saving the Crusade: The High Cost of Our Environmental Future" originally appeared in *Harper's Magazine*, January 1972.

"Business and Technology" from *Labor Technology and Productivity*, edited by Jules Backman, New York University Press. Copyright © 1974 by New York University. Reprinted by permission of The Bobbs-Merrill Company, Inc.

"Multinationals and Developing Countries: Myths and Realities" originally appeared in *Foreign Affairs*, October 1974.

"What Results Should You Expect? A Users' Guide to MBO" reprinted from *Public Administration Review*, January/February 1976. © 1976 by The American Society for Public Administration, 1225 Connecticut Avenue, N.W., Washington, D.C. All rights reserved. Reprinted by permission.

"The Coming Rediscovery of Scientific Management" originally appeared in *Conference Board Record*, June 1976. © 1976 by The Conference Board, Inc. Reprinted by permission of The Conference Board Record.

"The Bored Board" from the *Wharton Magazine*, Vol. I, #1, Fall 1976. © 1976 by The Wharton School of the University of Pennsylvania. Reprinted with permission.

"After Fixed Age Retirement Is Gone" from *The Future of Business*, edited by Max Ways for the Center of Strategic Studies, Georgetown University, Pergaman, 1978. © 1978 by Georgetown University, Washington, D.C. Reprinted by permission of the Center for Strategic and International Studies.

"Science and Industry: Challenges of Antagonistic Interdependence" originally appeared in *Science*, May 25, 1979.

"How to Guarantee Non-performance" reprinted from *Public Administration Review*, March/April 1980 under the title "The Deadly Sins in Public Administration." © 1980 by The American Society for Public Administration, 1225 Connecticut Avenue, N.W., Washington, D.C. All rights reserved. Reprinted by permission.

"Behind Japan's Success" originally appeared in *Harvard Business Review*, January/February 1981 under the title "Japan Inc., Myths & Realities."

"A View of Japan Through Japanese Art" from *Song of the Brush*, Catalogue of the Sansō Exhibition, Seattle Art Museum, 1979. Copyright © 1979 by Peter F. Drucker. Reprinted by permission.

# INDEX

dissent, informed, and MBO, 90–91
Doering, Otto, 101
domestic-content policy, developing
    countries, 69
Du Pont Co., 79, 174

early warning system, on technology
    impacts, 56
economic policy, Japan, 168–171
economics
    approaches to next, 17–18
    Classic, 5
    Keynesian influence on, 1–3
    and macro-economy, 16
    Mercantilism, 4
    and micro-economics, 14–16
    and national government, 17–18
    Neo-Classic, 5
    and Physiocrats, 3, 4–5
    rational expectations school, 2
    and Theory of Value, 5, 19–20
economist, and technology, 57
economist-king, and Keynesian
    economic policy, 12
economy. See also economics; world
    economy and productivity,
    Taylor's view, 103–104
Edison, Thomas Alva, 40, 44
education
    and environmental crisis, 26
    on environmental needs, 35
    explosion, and estrangement of
        science and industry, 151–152
    policy and priorities, developing
        countries, 85
    and university board of directors,
        111–112, 113, 117
effort, splintering, and non-performance,
    158–159
electrical industry, technology and
    lead time, 44–45
employees
    part-time, and retirement, 134–136
    relations with company, Japan,
        176–177
    and scientific management, 103–106

entropy, law of, 47
environment
    crisis, and emphasis on growth and
        industrial output, 24–27
    and incentives to reach goals, 27
    as issue in Japan, 173
    paying costs of cleaning, 23–24
    and pesticides, 33
    and punitive legislation, 27
    and technology, 22
    and Third World, 31–32
    and Union Carbide plant, 30
    where to start cleanup, 34–35
experience, failing to learn from,
    161–162
exporting, developing countries, 69–70
extractive industries, and developing
    countries, 62, 63

feedback
    and learning from experience, 162
    and performance measurement,
        89–90
firm theory, and profit maximization, 14
Follett, Mary Parker, 91, 181
Ford, Henry, 101
Ford Motor Co.
    and Edsel, 86
    and seat belts, 56
foreign exchange, and developing
    countries, 69
foremanship, functional, 100, 106
Franklin National Bank, 110
Friedman, Milton, 7, 12
Friedrich, Caspar David, 202
functional foremanship, and scientific
    management, 100, 106

General Accounting Office, 87
goals
    concentration, and communication, 84
    MBO, 93
government. See also public service
    organizations
    funding of research, 149–150
    doubts about science, 145

management (*continued*)
   and innovative organization, 47–49
   Japanese women in, 173
   what it is and should be, 90–96
Management by Objectives (MBO),
     79–81. *See also* management;
     non-performance; productivity;
     scientific management
   goal-setting, 93
   and performance measurement, 88–90
   popularity in government, 79–81
   and priorities, 84
   what management is and should be,
     90–96
   what objectives are and should be,
     81–90
managers
   from developing countries,
     training, 71
   role in developing countries, 64
   and technology, 39
   of technology, businessmen as, 44–45
March of Dimes, 164
Marcuse, Herbert, 59
Marietta, Ohio, and Union Carbide
   environmental pollution, 30
Marshall, Alfred, 15–16
   and Theory of Value, 19–20
Marx, Karl, 5–6, 8–9
   and law of diminishing productivity
     of capital, 47
   and technology, 59
matrix organization, and scientific
   management, 100, 106
Mayo Medical Clinic, 101, 106
*Medieval Technology and Social Change*
   (White), 58
membership, board of directors,
   119–123
mental work, and scientific
   management, 106–107
mercantilism, 4
micro-economics
   and Classics versus Marxists, 5–6
   and Kennedy tax cut, 11

   and Next Economics, 14–16
   and Physiocrats, 4–5
middle management, and computers,
   52–53
Midvale Steel Co., 101
Mill, John Stuart, 5
Ministry of International Trade and
   Industry, Japan (MITI), 168
   and automobile industry, 169–171
Mitsubishi group, 175
Monet, Claude, 197
money
   multiplier impact, and development,
     66–67
   transnational, 17
Montgomery Ward Co., 132
Morgan, Arthur, 159
Morikage, Kusumi, 186
Moscow, air pollution, 28
motivation, and scientific management, 98
multinationals. *See also* Industry
   assumptions about, 61–62
   board of directors, 113
   extractive industries, 62, 63
   global strategy, and developing
     countries, 68–72
   importance of developing countries to,
     62–64
   multiplier effect of money, 67
   and ownership of companies in
     developing countries, 72–74
   ownership versus control by, 74–75
   and world economy, 75–77
multiplier, and productive resources,
   developing countries, 70–71
multiplier impact, money, and
   development, 66–67
Mumford, Lewis, 58
Mundell, Robert, 2, 16
Murasaki Shikibu, Lady, 203

Nakane, Chie, 184
Nanga school, 186, 187, 194
national economies, and world
   economy, 16–17

National Health Service, British, 82, 158
national interest, and business policy,
     Japan, 171–173
national sovereignty, and environmental
     pollution, 31–32
Nestlé, 71
Nijō Castle, 188
Nobutada, Konoe, 199
non-performance. *See also* Management
     by Objectives (MBO); productivity
   and assumption of immortality,
        163–164
   and applying untested theories,
        160–161
   and failing to learn from experience,
        161–162
   and inability to abandon, 162–164
   and lofty objectives, 157–158
   and overstaffing, 159–160
   public service organizations, lack of
        concern about, 165–166
   and splintering effort, 158–159
Northrup Corp., 111

objectives. *See also* Management by
        Objectives (MBO)
   lofty, and non-performance, 157–158
   what they are and should be, 81–90
Office of Technology Assessment, 50, 54
Okyo, Maruyama, 186
organization
   board of directors, 112–115
   innovative, 46–49
   structure, and MBO, 94–95
overstaffing, and non-performance,
        159–160
ownership, of multinational branches,
        74–75

paper industry, as technology prone, 41
Parsons, Talcott, 59
participation, and MBO, 93
part-time employees, and retirement,
        134–136
Penn Central Railroad, 110

pension funds, and corporate
     ownership, 121
pension plans
   public sector, 138–139
   and retirement, 127
Pension Reform Act, 121
performance, measurement, and MBO,
     88–90
Perkins, Frances, 161
personality, development, and scientific
     management, 99
personnel decisions, and MBO, 94
pesticides, and environment, 33
pharmaceutical companies
   profitability, and developing
        countries, 63
   and regulation of new high-potency
        drugs, 56
physical resources, and productivity, 13
physical strain, and scientific
     management, 99
Physiocrats, 3, 4–5
planning, and anticipating technology,
     40–43
polarities, and tension, Japan, 188–191
police department, what objectives are
     and should be, 82–83
pollution, and technology, 22
population explosion
   and technology, 51
   and wire screen, 22, 51
posteriorities, and timing of priorities,
     85–86
poverty areas, and environmental
     crisis, 26
power companies, and regulation to cut
     air pollution, 55
prediction, difficulty of, 53–54
*Principles of Scientific Management*
     (Taylor), 99
priorities, and MBO, 84–87
private flying boom, prediction of,
     51–52
production, deemphasis, and
     unemployment, 25–26

science
    and antitrust bias, 147–149
    attitude of responsibility, 154–156
    dangers of drift from industry,
        152–154
    doubts about, 143–145
    estrangement from industry, 149–152
    and tax effects and industrial
        investment, 146–147
scientific management. *See also*
        management; Management by
        Objectives (MBO); productivity
    and mental work, 106–107
    myths about, 97
    principles, 98–100
    and productivity, 100–102
    and quality of life, 102–103
    and worker, 103–106
Scientific Revolution, Keynesian, and
        productivity, 9
Sears, Roebuck & Co., 72, 101
    mission, 88
second careers, and retirement, 140–141
self-control, and MBO, 93
Sengai, Gibon, 189–190, 201
senility, and retirement, 131
services and activities, candidates for
        abandonment, 86
sewage treatment, and technology,
        22, 25
Shackle, G.L.S., 15
Shapiro, Irving, 174
Shibuzawa, Eiichi, 172, 173, 179–180
Shijō school, 186
Shinto, 191–192, 196
*Shop Management* (Taylor), 98
Siemens, 39, 40, 44
Sierra Club, 25
Simpson's of Canada, 72
Singer, Charles, 58
Sloan, Alfred P. Jr., 79
Social Security, and retirement, 127,
        137–138
Society for the History of
        Technology, 58

Sociologists, and technology, 59
Sōtatsu, Tarawaya, 187–188
Soviet Union, prepackaged
        technology, 153
Special Drawing Rights (SDRs), 17
    and multinationals, 76
stagflation, 10–11
standards, for retirement, 129–132
steel industry, as technology prone, 41
Stockholm, beaches polluted by
        Leningrad sewage, 28
strategies, and MBO, 88
strip mining, and environment, 23
structure
    of innovative organization, 49
    and MBO, 94–95
success, and environmental crisis, 28
supply
    and government deficits, 11
    and Mercantilism, 4
    and Next Economics, 13
survivors, and retirement, 128

targets, and MBO, 87
"Task Study" (Taylor), 9
taxes, and investment, industry, 146–147
Taylor, Frederick Winslow, 9
    and scientific management, 97–107
teamwork, and scientific
        management, 101
*Technics and Civilization* (Mumford), 58
technology
    anticipating and planning, 40–43
    and business, 37–40
    and difficulty of prediction, 53–54
    and environment, 22
    history of, 57–59
    and innovative organization, 46–49
    need for monitoring, 54–56
    pace of, 44–45
    prepackaged, 153
    responsibility for impact of, 49–53
*Technology and Culture*, 58
*Technology in Western Civilization*
        (Kranzberg and Pursell), 58